The
Decline
of
Christianity
and the
Rise of the
Pastor/Priests
in America

John Morton

WESTBOW
PRESS®
A DIVISION OF THOMAS NELSON
& ZONDERVAN

WestBow Press books may be ordered through booksellers or by contacting:

WestBow Press
A Division of Thomas Nelson & Zondervan
1663 Liberty Drive
Bloomington, IN 47403
www.westbowpress.com
1 (866) 928-1240

ISBN: 978-1-5127-7122-0 (sc)
ISBN: 978-1-5127-7123-7 (e)

Library of Congress Control Number: 2017900130

Print information available on the last page.

WestBow Press rev. date: 06/01/2017

Contents

Note on Quotations and Abbreviations

All Scripture quotations are taken from various orthodox versions of the Holy Bible. NT and OT will occasionally be used for Old and New Testament. Quotations identified as MLE or Penguin refer to the Modern Library Edition and Penguin edition of Edward Gibbon's Decline and Fall of the Roman Empire.

To the Late

Kent Mathews

The passionate seeker of Christian community, the wise professor's earnest librarian, that individual in Bonhoeffer's Life Together, the lover of the French language, the companion of the Palestinian laborer, Colorado's exemplar at home and afar, though bedecked in death with flowers from the disabled, alive as a voice to my conscience, my dearest brother of the Psalms,

This book is dedicated

Historical Introduction

The unbridled attack I have made on the practical heresy of American church leadership is made on the shoulders of others. Edward Gibbon in his Decline and Fall of the Roman Empire protested against a similar type of misleadership long before I did. No doubt that if the fourth century priests had read Gibbon's analysis of themselves they would have made a similar cry as our own contemporary pastor/priests do, "But you go too far. We are only human!" Certainly Gibbon's reply would be that religious history has a say in the matter, or with a quotation from the New Testament. When a house is on fire it does not burn quietly, but groans loudly before it bursts into flame. That groan is this little work against the soft clothed orators of the Western and American church leadership.

But I can explain my task in greater detail. If this book is to be taken seriously, it cannot be what everybody else is saying, i.e., 'some things should change,' holding on to certain things while casting aside others, when the blood must be entirely renewed. So if one were to approach the matter that a pint of new blood now and again is enough, when it is ALL the bloo⟨ that is poisoned, then I have to make sure that I do not say l⟨

the others that some things should change-for then I would be as compromised as the well-healed western clerical hoard. No, the authentic warning that springs out of Gibbon and that I attempt to note from my own experience and New Testament criticism is given in such a way that it leaves no question as to what must be done. Like the doctor who rushes into the room of a comatose patient-this is the intended impact: the doors fly open and there he strides, fixated on the eyes of the patient. First confusion, then resignation-and then the doctor bursts in.

This is what I intend to show in the ensuing chapters. And you can know for certain that I am all too familiar with the lack in the pastorate, that it is mediocre, that it lets itself off the hook by saying that it is only human, that it does not desire real transformation, least of all in themselves. But as a falcon preens its wings so there is not a feather out of place, aeronautically so designed that it falls from the sky like a beam of light, as such the falcon does not take flight if one plume should stick out, so does this book recoil from the "some things should change." I should have a little knowledge of this by now, having lived almost my entire adult life in some fashion connected to the conformed church.

Yet I am the last one to say the book demands all or nothing. Either we imitate Gibbon's description of the early church or. . . secularism. No, and no again. Honesty is the crucial word that marks this work. O that an honest confession would roll off the tongue of Western clerics. Honesty is what is demanded first and foremost, not all or nothing, though that is what I 'll be misrepresented as saying. Yes, mere honesty is what opens the castle door. But what is it that blocks every hope of heaven? It is this 'some things should change,' which the demonic adores, or it is triviality, or a sneaky cunning, all of which brings evangelicalism back to the fourth century, and that is what Gibbon (and later Kierkegaard) rails against. Honesty is what we propose. And it is in a cemetery, when a widow visits her husband's grave, whispering to him, acting as if his life depended upon her presence, however much she may think him at her side, he is not there, not physically present. So is this 'some things should change' a delusion. Only honesty grasps what must be done. And the long hard look I have taken at the robotic clergy will show the fantastic liberties that that leadership has taken, with regard to the truth, which would certainly tempt any sincere religious to say to these long-robed well-spoken children of privilege 'all or nothing.' But that is not what is first demanded. Honesty as regards the massive mediocrity that they have allowed themselves to be involved in, then on to the early church.

Gibbon remarks somewhere that the primitive Christians were not known so much by their outward signs-the signs of the cross and the fish etc.-but by their refusal to recognize other gods, their austerity and self-denial, which was an expression of the fact that they served Christianity AND that they sought to imitate the episcopate which led the way. All this we-need-only-to-build-an-addition-and-to-modernize-our-hymnbooks sort of thinking subverts Christianity, and enhances itself, and will never amount to anything but perhaps gain a stamp of approval from the local zoning board; but what gains the eternal stamp is an honest admission.

In this respect and in that of the collision between the early church leadership and the current, one cannot help but notice the iron clad influence of Soren Kierkegaard, whose writings I have not yet fully plumbed, such is the well of everlasting nourishment, courage, challenge and above all, leniency, in his work. It is Gibbon though who gives us the historical and incremental seduction of the integrity of the early church. In the interest of paltriness this seduction has cunningly made its way into the present age, disguised to some degree, yet strikingly similar. We note the weeds, without neglecting the most luxuriant wheat.

I dare call this effort a work of love for the church. It is sincerely done in order to draw the church back to integrity and beauty, and it is my desire that one who reads it might be won for Christ and His committed church. That is our venture. Whether or not our book becomes popular is not our business; our effort does not become less disinterested because there are too few readers.

The Real Issue and to Whom this is Addressed

The churches were filled with the increasing multitude of these unworthy converts [the polytheists], who had conformed from temporal motives to the reigning religion (p. 531 MLE) (italics mine).

The worldly church, what church leaders call church, is a terrible inversion, a complete reversal of the New Testament. There is not the slightest desire to resemble it. These real champions of faith-the Grahams, Dobson, Warren, Osteen, Jakes, Meyers, Yancey, etc. are merely a part of a long line of the doctrinally correct yet heretical in practice, going back seventeen hundred years. This is easy to show-a glance at the first chapter of Luke will do. Yet this is not the heart of the problem. The trouble is that the New Testament's take on what it means to be a Christian just does not blend well with the notion that Christianity adds a little tobasco sauce to life-don't forget a pinch of personal morality-but is a full-out attack on his drives and instincts, aiming to reign them in. Christ calls this an offence, a scandal, and a stumbling block. It is why Christianity never makes strides among the comfortable and why western evangelical leaders do not understand it and what's worse do not want to, conjuring up a horde of excuse that always and inevitably lead to ignoring wars and the poor, or simply shoo the New Testament away by the help of lies and lofty sermons saying its Christianity they preach. But it isn't. Then they sing Amazing Grace to what is not Christianity.

What Christianity IS about is getting people to see that Christianity runs up against our very nature, that to become a Christian means voluntary pain that will lead to suffering, self-denial, bouts with self-doubt because confrontation is such an every day part of life (also known as prophetic love). But these so-called orthodox have turned Christianity into a tra-la-la-we-are-under-grace-religion conducted by the pastor/song leader. Agonies await the comfortable. Greater agonies await the minister who led them to believe they could enter heaven without voluntary suffering (not the suburban definition of suffering but the New Testament's). Even greater agonies are for those who serve as the minister's lackeys, who take him as their example and lick his boots, hovering about him like adoring teen girls, matching anything the eunuchs from the fourth century Roman or Persian empires could offer. When I say this suburbanites get upset, if that's possible among such enormous numbers of those at ease in the land. It does not matter, for their gut reaction is entirely irrelevant. If I should care about their feelings that matters even less. Put simply: They are not going to applaud when I show them that Christianity means beginning a journey that resembles the sufferings of Christ, particularly the comfortable. So, they become angry and withdraw, and that is exactly what the NT says will happen again and again. When chubby fellow stands in front of me as I preach outside the

New Life megamillion dollar church complex, he insisting the buildings are needed to save souls, while a woman three feet away is attempting to distract me until Security arrives, well, from the New Testament's point of view I am doing something right, no matter how ridiculous the whole situation looks.

The gospel of suffering is there for the poor. When in France I lived and worked in a village dedicated to the handicapped. There I came to know Joseph, a middle-aged man who had lived among a number of severely disabled folk for a decade. We never had more than a few brief talks yet it was easy to see in him both seriousness and merriness. He had helped many and was no doubt troubled by the burden, yet he laughed easily. Of course there are thousands-not millions-of others like Joseph sacrificing for no apparent earthly reason and my little work is not directed at them. They are Christians and they are alone, because their orthodox friends don't have the courage to join them, or do something similar. They understand this, that their evangelical friends would rather not join them, thank you very much.

Looking for someone to blame? Place it at the feet of Pastor Dimm. The charge? Treason against Christianity by this comfortable imbecile who is guilty of fraud-his goal was to get himself a crowd, and Christianity was given a back seat. His method? Use greed, power and image to his advantage, make it quietly clear these things are there for the taking in the church, be certain these matters are not applied to himself or his church and if they are use Bible commentary to confuse things. This is the trick to packing or at least aiming to pack the churches.

But the pastor's idea of Christianity is not the church

Christ, which knows that the New Testament stands with iron strength against our passions. Where it is taught correctly and lived out there are no mass conversions and little money. What makes the real Christian different from the typical Protestant or Catholic is that the Christian has made an honest confession that his is not the Christianity of the NT and that so-help-him-God he will do something about it. Here is where the divide begins with popular evangelicalism, where the Christian begins to act contrary to his own passions. Crucially, he also begins to act contrary to the consuming passions of popular evangelicalism. What would naturally attract him, the splendid little chapel amid the hills of golden autumns is left behind for the core city which is full of the poor and the victim. Then he commits himself to it. He does this inspite of the place that little chapel holds in his heart. He does this inspite of being misunderstood, ignored, or even admired by the little chapel on the hill. This action the priestly and clerical hoard cannot stand, figuring it to be such a threat to their lifestyles something has to be done. What to do? Appeal to the natural passions of men of course. That, or ignore the sincere Christian altogether and work up a lather about gay marriage or evolution etc.-but they make sure its a safe topic that secular society either condemns already or does not care much about.

But the Christian stands his ground on what at first does not please him a whole lot. Now, alas, this also has to be said. I take no joy in arguing vehemently that now, in our generation it is ime for Christians to no longer use the term evangelical. The ·m, so Biblically rooted and so rich in history, so wonderfully connected in times past with constructive action, has to go for now. Evangelicals (I include myself) have to their eternal criminality so altered and ruined its meaning (the bearer of Good News), so blasphemously mixing it with politics that evangelicalism now bears an impossible double meaning: one who bears the Good News AND a political agenda. Evangelical leadership have no one but themselves to blame for turning a golden word into a profane association. Now every missionary knows that the Bible allows for a certain degree of contextualization, of flexibility in how words are used. They know there is no need to offend in lesser matters, as in the use of highly charged words. In Egypt I learned to be discerning in my vocabulary around Muslims. For conservative Islamists, the Crusades might as well have been yesterday so better not identify myself as a Christian, rather a follower of Jesus, a term that carries less historical pain for the Muslim and can open a dialogue. This is a NT application.

In the West let the Christians call themselves Christians, with all the seriousness that that involves. Likewise, let evangelicals call themselves evangelicals, then everyone will know they stand more or less with the status quo. Most American church pastors when they read this will go berserk, how he and his congregation are Christians too and do not let anyone say otherwise, that there is no difference between a Christian and an evangelical etc. etc. Technically of course the pastors are correct. But my veteran detective is building a case of fraud and sees Rev. Dimm as a person of interest, perhaps remembering Shakespeare's 'I think you protest too much,' he approaches Dimm after his rousin sermon and compliments him on his speaking skills, saying has a little problem he needs help with, that as hard as he looks he can find no evidence of New Testament Christianity in his life. Now Dimm, feeling ambushed, is suddenly angry. 'This very afternoon I visit the sick,' he says, 'and tomorrow I do a wedding and a funeral on the same day. On Tuesday there's a Bible study then I lead a marriage and family seminar. Christ dwells in the heart, sir. What do you want from me? If you want more evidence than my shepherding this church then look at Jesus' life and that is enough for me.' Dimm walks away in a huff.

Our detective is left standing. A woman who has been listening glares at him, says 'That's right' then leaves. The detective, like any good detective, had anticipated Dimm's answer. Sure he was hoping, just this once, that he would get a confession. But no. He smiles to himself and returns home to compare notes on Dimm's life, which he will use with a NT and a newspaper that he will submit to a grand jury for indictment. His conclusions: That Rev. Dimm isn't lying, he actually does what he says he does. The crime lies in that what he does just doesn't agree much with the book he says he imitates in the pulpit. He visits the sick. Volunteers do the same but the Rev. receives a good salary. He presides at weddings and funerals. The state will do the same and for less the price. Bible studies and seminars, if the pastor is truly serious, must be done where the participants can truly see day-to-day what the pastor is talking about. Otherwise it is just another two hour a week wonder whose meaning disappears over the course of time. However, what truly aggravates the crime, turns it into the first degree his use of the last two chapters of the book of Ephesians to justify evangelical family life-the suburban home, technologies and gadgets, two or more cars, a must-have-a-child-of-my-own mentality, immoral jobs-this while only looking at how the family communicates with each other.

The grand jury returns the indictment: enough evidence to bring charges for aggravated assault on the church of Christ.

The detective testifies that he has seen the New Testament lived out, that it is not just stuck in time, that this collective mass of perjurers-the priests, pastors, and preachers-has no excuse. He says there are a few exceptions. When asked who they are he looks angrily, with a touch of sadness, at Dimm, who sits with his head in his Bible, then replies that there are individuals and small groups who admit to God, themselves and others that they have failed in the most important task of their lives, received mercy, now at peace seeking to do for others what was done for them, then Dimm seeing himself let off the hook by this last comment by the detective, sighs in relief. Yet our detective goes on. He says the sincere church, precisely by accepting this offer of mercy, has committed itself to Christ, thus breaking with the ever-changing morality of the masses to follow Him in a way that is concrete, practical, and visible. So faith distinguishes the sincere, a faith that expresses itself in collision with the general public and the insincere church. The detective says he rarely sees the New Testament in action in North America or Europe, but in poor nations he sees it frequently. His investigations have discovered that, as in Dimm's congregation, a Christian has come to be defined as anyone who says they are (Dimm is now squirming). Thus the only way to determine who the Christi really is, says the detective, is to return to the New Testament to recover the definition, which is: (1) who you are (2) what you do and how you do it and (3) in this age of luxury, where you live. He gives as an example, a badly neglected neighborhood in Columbia Heights, Washington D.C., two miles from the White House. There they meet in each other's homes, break bread, share, forbid military support, and strive to live out the meaning of the gospel of suffering and joy. Their presence is highlighted against the congregations that surround them in the middle class and suburban neighborhoods of D.C., and particularly against the Congressional prayer groups and most of all the President's own religious circle.

The detective now pales and looks down at the ground. 'I accuse myself first of all,' he says, 'for not doing enough to prevent the crime, for holding back and not getting in earlier among the church leadership for reasons of Christian subversion, for I had all this information that I did nothing with.' Then he looks up and his face reddens as he stares at Dimm, who has returned to leafing through his Bible. 'You have, because you have loved only yourself and only your kind, abandoned Christ's demands,' claims the detective, 'of bringing the convert into an entirely neighborhood, where he is instructed and taught, then sent out. Instead, you let your congregation think that their loneliness was Christianly normal, that the building as a meeting place a couple times a week was Christianly normal, that their comfortable suburban routine was the same as being in the world and not of it, that they can work anywhere they want and say a Christian calling, that allowing their sons and daughters to become soldiers which is automatically to hate your enemy, was Christianly normal, that having your own children was better than adopting, not saying anything about what Christ or James said about orphans. You let them think that those words about the poor always being with you meant that a whole coliseum of children around the globe had to die every day, and that this was Christianly normal. You did not utter a word against social media and gadgets, leaving them to think that by them you have Christian fellowship, when in fact they deeply wound the face-to-face communion of Christians, which is the definition of church.

You will be held accountable for these things, and let God himself judge between us. Yet inspite of everything there was one thing you could have done, just one word you could have uttered which would have meant you were a true Christian pastor. You could have read before the congregation St. Paul's words, that 'if we have hope only in this life, we are more than anyone, to be pitied.' You could have stood quietly a few minutes while people came to understand its meaning, which would lead to nervous fidgeting. You could have said 'Unlike Paul we have lived as if there were only one life, this one, and so we have no reason at all to be pitied, living as comfortably as we do. That what we have lived is in fact a caricature, a parody, a playing at Christianity that Paul calls a lie. This I as your pastor and we as a congregation admit and confess. Now may Christ have mercy upon us.' This is the beginning of all Christian action and what the pious Hebrew calls a breakthrough. But you refused to say this. So I can say no more except to warn you, warn you until you have been warned enough of the eternal consequences of not making that confession.

Dimm is searching hard now in his Bible while the detective makes a move toward the door where a couple people are waiting anxiously for him. There is a larger crowd waiting for Dimm, chanting their support.

Our parable does not say what the detective does next. But the committed Christian knows what is next. This for him does not boil down to doctrine, doctrine,and more doctrine, but a changed life, and that has to be visible.

When at Fuller Seminary over three decades ago we watched an ongoing debate between the missions and theology professors that continues to this day. Missions argued that conversions were more critical than bearing one's cross and obeying the commandments Christ sets forth, that a missionary's first goal is conversion. Then, after conversion is achieved, the missionary can start working on the conditions attached to that conversion. Say a pagan king with ten wives converts to Christianity. He is allowed to keep his wives while slowly but surely led to choose one. Though there is no guarantee he will give them up, this is the goal of the missionary. Theology teachers said otherwise, arguing that the king had to be told from the outset that if he were to convert he must choose one wife. His choosing monogamy was a condition of conversion.

I cannot stress enough here that I met many missionaries at Fuller who held luxury in contempt, leaving for miserable hovels all over the globe to preach Christ crucified, who just like myself were not savvy enough theologically to grasp the full implications of the missionary professors' teaching. Yet they lived and spoke decisively enough to let the American church know what it meant to become a Christian.

The theology department easily knocked down this notion of conversion without change, and the more mature Christians at the seminary knew it. But good theology there and elsewhere failed and continues to fail to gain a convincing victory for one simple reason: missionaries live more like Christians, among the poor, than theology professors who live comfortably. So what does it mean for young Mark, after taking a youth pastoral position at Bel Air Presbyterian church near Hollywood, but to admire the missionary then humbly and eventually accept the swimming pool just like his theology professor.

Then our esteemed professor would, when pressed, say something ridiculous to justify his participation in what he knew to be a worldly church. The best excuse I heard was that the established church was the only one we have. Running a close second was that we cannot challenge it because it is our wonderful privilege to be there as untrained pastoral interns etc. I can recall my own less than stellar ministerial debut. Just after being released as a youth pastor from a church for saying nuclear weapons were a sin, my seminary advisor sent me to speak with one of the more left-leaning ministers to see if he could draw me back into the fold, or at least exist on the edge of it. The minister gave up the attempt after an hour. But I had already given up on myself a year before, for I knew then I was lost to the conformed church forever.

The seminary was only acting as an extension of the church. To look at the professors as examples is as absurd as looking at middle-class-pastors-on-up as examples, busy as they are working, ever working, to increase numbers in their churches. They think that by having a crowd it will encourage the faith of the individual, that a glance at the masses will build individual strength and maturity. But this is a disastrous view from the standpoint of Christianity. Certainly when an individual is instructed in Christianity as a way of life, which can only be done when people are living within walking distance of each other and in neighborhoods of need, then strength is added to strength and you have a Christian church. But most evangelical pastors have reversed this, and in the case of the megachurch this weakness increases to the second power. We think of India, where a couple of children are forced to marry. Weakness wedded to weakness. This describes the megachurch perfectly, a partnership of immaturity and spiritually unprepared.

There are exceptions in places of poverty and need, and this little work is not addressed to those who have applied New Testament teachings to their lives and live near enough to each other to be that primitive church. There that little building they call church is really unnecessary because they already are the Christian church, housing the vulnerable, confronting local principalities and powers like weapons test sites, Wal-Mart's low wages, a toxic plant or rising housing costs. Those Christians in these neighborhoods know by now they risk being overwhelmed with the wounded and underwhelmed with experienced Christians nearby so they will be tempted to flee to the middle class or suburbs. The gospel aims at halting such a move.

This is what happened to our house church in Denver's core

city in the eighties. The absence of trained Christians, which would have meant decisive servant leadership, led to decisions that were taken democratically, where even new converts had an equal say. Thus our little church fell apart for lack of a solid foundation. Then, as was expected, the majority of those folks were slowly absorbed, in lifestyle and commitment, back into quietly conformed middle class churches.

This humble piece is meant for those who have put on their running shoes and are braced to run after a man like Phillip, who said 'Come and see,' or those who dream to, or those who are asking for another chance. For those who do not, who are satisfied with the status quo and are not ashamed at all of American church leadership, I only ask that you continue to describe yourselves as evangelicals-for it gets confusing if you describe yourselves as Christians-then be happy that you are anonymous or barely known among your church. Rejoice that now you can dress up Christianity in a suit, tie, or long robe and go on enjoying the American dream.

American Evangelical Authorities: Beyond Human Ambition

'The successful candidate [to the episcopate] is secure that he will be enriched by the offerings of matrons; that as soon as his dress is composed with becoming care and elegance, he may proceed. . .and the sumptuousness of the Imperial table will not equal the profuse and delicate entertainments [he receives] . . . How much more rationally [would they] consult their true happiness ...[if] they would imitate the exemplary life of some provincial bishops, whose temperance and sobriety, whose mean apparel and downcast looks, recommend their pure and modest virtue to the Deity and his true worshipers' (Ammainus, p. 480 MLE) (italics mine).

A Biblical rule for how close a pastor is to Christ: The more worldly beauty points to him as Christlike, the farther he is from Him. Conversely: The lesser the appearances, the closer he is to Christ. Think of Christ's own life. The incidents that grab our attention in the gospels are His birth and death, where there was nothing to admire (barnyard animals, naked men nailed to wood on a well-viewed hill). Yet God was present when He seemed

He could not be. Now when did Christ walk away from others? When they wanted to make Him a king.

Historically the pastorate has been close to Christ when their little flocks had, from persecution, to meet in catacombs and cemetaries, gather quietly in homes, were sent to jail, run out of town, go into hiding or made to suffer. Christ was near. Then came power, so much power, power at the side of emperors and kings and the greater the power the farther away God was. For Christ's presence can generally be determined by who and what surrounds us most of the time. The more fabulous and artificial our worship environment is, the less God is there. Where there is great worldly show, Christ is absent.

The early church knew all this and thus communion was shared only among those it knew to be faithful and humble. But with ascending numbers and power came communion to every Tom, Dick and Harry that wanted it, and Christ was absent. When pastors had side jobs, were, like Paul, tentmakers, when they refused salaries so as not to be a burden to their flocks, Christ was nearer than when ministerial salaries, good salaries, bigger and bigger salaries arose. And since these salaries are an expression of externals, of image, numbers and power, Christ makes himself increasingly scarce:

The whole body of the Catholic [or Christian] clergy, more numerous perhaps than the legions, was exempted by the emperors from all service, private or public, all munincipal offices, and all personal taxes and contributions which pressed on their fellow-citizens with intolerable weight; (p. 396 MLE) (italics mine).

This explains how America's privileged ministers have come, inch by wretched inch, to be as they are. Another way of looking at it is the steady dismissal of Christ by introducing niceties like fine buildings, long robes and high sounding titles. Mix that in with a stupefying arsenal of theology, commentaries, and doctrine and these ministers have succeeded, in their prestige, in hiding Him away in a dark corner.

Say this to your esteemed minister and he will surely answer 'but you don't know my ministry and the presence of the Holy Spirit in our church. We have a teaching ministry (Fine-so as to train one in burying the truth) and we have an evangelism committee (Fine-so as to train one in burying the truth) and I am asking God to bring more people into leadership positions so I can delegate more authority (Fine-so as to train one in burying the truth). We even have a missions committee' etc.

A thousand times no! It is nothing more than a multiplication of the spiritually weak. To grow in faith is precisely to ignore this perjured (upon ordination they dedicate themselves to the New Testament) gang of middle class and suburban pastors and leave them to exercise their oratorical brilliance in empty sanctuaries. Before ignoring him though you are free, as a Christian and as an adult to laugh out loud once when the pastor makes some outrageous identification with the gospel. Perhaps he reads that God chose the weak things of the world to shame the strong. This he says from the pulpit of a well appointed sanctuary. Now you are free to laugh loud enough to make the people around you nervous and wonder if you are mad, and to show the pastor there is at least one who understands, one who has not allowed himself to be tricked into believing the pastor is serious about following Christ in simplicity.

Knock, and the door will be opened to you. The law of Christ is not complex: The more your life is tied to the imitation of Christ the more you will come into conflict with worldly clergy. This imitation you seek, which is the same as pulling down idols within the church, leads you into that conflict which evangelicals keep talking about but never really enter into. Yet this conflict is exactly what it means to trust God, to move faithfully inspite of it. Set out on this journey of faithful confrontation and He will accompany you, just as He did a man who confronted the inactivity of the church sixteen hundred years ago:

The pathetic representations [of the gladiatorial arena] of Prudentius [a Christian poet] were less effectual than the general boldness of Telemachus, an Asiatic monk, whose death was more useful to mankind than his life. The Romans were provoked by the interruption of their pleasures; and the rash monk, who had descended into the arena to separate the gladiators, was overwhelmed under a shower of stones. But the madness of the people soon subsided; they respected the memory of Telemachus, who had deserved the honors of martyrdom; and they submitted without a murmur to the laws of Honorius, which abolished forever the human sacrifices of the amphitheater (p. 554 MLE) (italics mine).

We must at least admire such courage, which the pastors will use in their sermons on Sunday (before the crowds) then promptly forget on Monday (before their colleagues).

We speak of crowds and recall these continual religious

political campaigns where Christ sits and watches. Then with an eye more expert than the jeweler who examines the diamond, He takes careful note of those who would use His name and words to gain political power. He also notes those who are not and are out there risking in truth. Those loving yet fearful eyes that scan the earth: Where is he? Where is she? In the meantime those pastors and priests asleep in the land are also risking, as long as there is something concrete in it-an audience, prestige, money, advancement and comfort. Yet His eyes search high and low for those who are sincerely risking, who have banked their hopes on the promises of God, and will act on no concrete reward. These are actions that evangelical authorities will inwardly despise because it exposes their own motives.

These misleaders much prefer constructing great buildings for God and congregation so as to create a proper atmosphere for worship. But the refined thief in front of the camera and behind the pulpit still preaches that God is spirit, while paying token attention to that poor Ethiopian, Iraqi, Afgani, who seeks the kingdom of God. That seeker is found and renewed in such a way that the reverend cannot and will not understand, for the seeker now has a more splendid time with his bread and tea than the pastor in the banquet hall eying the desserts. When Christ expresses Himself through an individual He first rids the individual of appearances, teaching him that the greater the image the less His presence. But rabbits will dig complex warrens and so church leaders will pile up their bricks as homage to the image. With most there is not a hint of revulsion when the pastor starts talking about a vision or a dream he had from the Lord for a new building, a structure that is a beacon for the city. No, even the educated masses who gather on Sunday, at enormous expense, thoroughly believe he is their leader and that he rightly interprets the will of God. Why? Because he so humbly calls on God's presence then proclaims the gospel. But he is not as he seems. Christ is far distant from the man who loves display.

From a secular perspective nothing can compare to the buffoonery of the ministerial upper class, though I have seen much in the way of political circus. Yet it is the pastoral class that adds the monkey riding the dog show, and it is just that show that puts them before Christ, front and center.

I remember in India a politician, one Laloo Yadov, famous for outrageous behaviour amid scandal. Yet he could not approach America's religious finest in robbery and foolishness. Yadov would show his love for the common man by occasionally riding in rikshaws, while our refined pastor drives up quietly in his BMW. Yadov holds conferences on overpopulation while he himself has ten children, just as the suburban priest condemns sexual promiscuity while taking in parish money that could be spent on responsible birth control around the globe. Yadov enriches himself by selling cattle fodder meant for farmers. The pastor sells the refined grandeur of his structure built from the savings of his hard working and trusting congregants.

What makes the monkey antics of the pastors so demonically worse is that like Yadov they will say they are helping people spiritually, but unlike him they do so in the name of Christ. Yes, Yadov pretends to befriend the poor, but he does not do it with a New Testament in hand. No, this is a scheme only our court flatterers thrive on. Even Judas did not do this in his final hours. The rich pastors who play-act as they betray Him. When it comes to true religion, the refined and secure American pastorate are a whole lot worse than cannibals, who do not feign friendship as they consume their victim.

What the Primitive Church's Judgment is About American Evangelicalism

We should naturally assume that so benevolent a doctrine [Christianity] would have been received with due reverence, even by the unbelieving world . . . The new converts seemed to renounce their family and country that they might connect themselves in an indissoluble band of union with a peculiar society which everywhere assumed a different character from the rest of mankind (p. 272-282 MLE).

The middle and upper middle class churches are nothing but beautiful counterfeits, thanks to the pastor/priests. The Christian churches through the first 300 years of the church's life give history the greatest example ever of the meaning of Christianity. The worldly church however, exists as a living, breathing violation of the first commandment. How exactly are these two churches, of two different ages, different?

When the early church formed, they would not budge in their faith and behaviour. Not our conformed pastors, who are just so eager to please. They guide a religious social club, using Christ for their own purposes in an American definition of a kingdom on earth instead of imitating Christ on earth. Their notion is

more or less the American dream. The early church rejected
Roman luxury. They knew if they accepted Roman standards
then it was no longer The church, which could be easily shown
by simply watching their actions. So the church stood its ground
against Roman idolatry, Caesar, the philosophers and the mob.
Now, when clerical leaders made compromises with America
on pivital matters, economy and military, Christianity was lost.

America's court flatterers assume that the conflict between
Christ and world has already been won. They fear that this
conflict could be lost by the erosion of morality in some places, loss
of religious freedoms, constitutional rights etc. But on the whole
they believe that Christianity is engrained into the American way
of life, church buildings are everywhere, evangelical politicians
are protecting us, the Bible formed our country and the founding
fathers were Christians. They call conflicts like homosexuality,
gay marriage, sexual integrity, abortion, creationism, family
unity, and media the real battleground now. But the big battles
(climate change, nuclear war) are shoved aside. And so we have
the American success story and the church united, which is in
no way connected to the Christ of the New Testament nor the
early church. Christ's love was met with hatred and attacks from
both the world and false believers, exactly what He foretold. The
early church believed Him, took on the conflict as inevitable and
critically, knew it could only survive in opposition.

Place Warren, Dobson, the Grahams, Osteen, Jakes, Hagee
and their clan in the early church and they would immediately
be subject to stern rebuke, excommunication and disfellowship.
Why? For praising Caesar for vile actions and offering incense

(conforming) under the Roman standard, for permitting and even encouraging profuse luxury, and aiding and abetting their converts in becoming soldiers. Turn it around and have members of the early church walk into a modern church building and watch them become disoriented as to just who and what is being worshiped. Then watch what happens next.

The early believers had such an abhorrence of idolatry that in order to keep themselves pure and undefiled they were given, on a daily basis, training. The convert learned what was clean and unclean. The number of deities and observances which were connected to private and public life, such as the circus, hippodrome, theater or marketplace, made it very demanding to engage in business or entertainment in Rome. One could find oneself with some unbelieving friends and suddenly an idol is invoked and a drink poured out to someone's happiness, or perhaps one's unbelieving father had died and as the procession advanced, his father's blood is poured out and water is sprinkled on the pallbearers. The Christian either had to protest or leave the scene immediately.

Serious Christians have these types of experiences living abroad. Say when they are stopped and alms are requested, in a slightly threatening voice, to support a mosque, temple, or religious festival. These requests are easy to reject. But what about the gifts of poor children, which we know to be offerings to idols? They are rejected too while tactfully claiming one's Christianity, for the stain of idolatry must be avoided.

The judgments of the first Christians against America's conformist leaders lie not just with sacrificing to idols, though they are guilty of that too. More with its loving embrace of the business of war, preparation for war, and government. They were offended by what the conformists now chase after. There was no swearing of oaths, taking part in the ceremonies of empire, or becoming active in political life. They could not be persuaded by a less perfect covenant (the Old Testament) that it was lawful to take human life either through the judicial system or a defensive war. The whole notion of the Just War, which the Stoics and philosophers defended, was repulsive to them. They understood government institutions to be necessary so they passively obeyed the pagan magistrates when they did not hinder the proclamation of the gospel. They took the NT passages on submission to authorities to mean an inactive part in either civil administration or military. Those who already held high positions in these places at the time of their conversion were told to either quit immediately or desert if soldiers (Tertullian), or perhaps given a grace period to do so. They were not and could not become government officials, soldiers or judges without giving up their Christian faith, even if their resistance was defined as harming the common good.

Of course this position of the early Christians led to the question that has been posed to serious Christians for two thousand years: What would happen to civilization if all of humanity were to assume the character of Christians? Evangelical leaders press this insulting question upon sincere young Christians to silence their enthusiasm and justify themselves. The answer the early Christian apologists often gave was 'they (pagans) know what is right for them.' In other words, doing something is better than doing nothing. This is what Ghandi meant when he said he would rather take up arms than be a passive observer to injustice. So the young man who rejects true Christianity, yet wishes to defend the oppressed may actually be taking a slightly progressive step (toward faith) by becoming a soldier, as opposed to inaction. If he survives that decision ethically and physically.

It should be noted that certain church fathers, like Origen, were occasionally consulted for diplomatic solutions to complex political problems. There were no Billy/Franklin Grahams among the church fathers though, who sang Hosannas to presidents as they spread the banner of the cross (as Constantine did for Rome) over American wars.

It has been argued that the first Christians withdrew from war, government and empire because they believed Christ would return soon so there was no need to get involved. Then, when He did not return as assumed, they became more realistic and thus political. But if pastoral authorities studied history instead of just reading their colleagues they would never have swallowed this idea that the Christians became political because Christ had not returned as planned. No doubt the first Christians thought Christ would return soon, being commanded to be ready by obedience. Indeed, they were anti-political. They had been commanded to be CONSTANTLY ready for His return. It was when they started crying Maranatha (Come Lord Jesus) ALONG WITH Hail Caesar that they gave up Christian realism for political fantasies. Also, when the early church made its longing for Christ's return clear, did they ever say they were the last generation of Christians to have that longing? Not among early church leaders, though they certainly hoped they were the last generation.

It was not giving up the hope of Christ's return that led to Christians becoming more 'realistic' and worldly. What was true was that by the end of the third century luxury had made significant progress into the austere lives of the Christians, who had been given a taste of the good life. So Christ's return was moved to the backburner, behind the pursuit of comfort. Now add the fact that the early church had experienced long lapses between persecutions and that meant the conflict between Christ and the Roman world was reduced. Thus their invincible courage, which had thrived under persecution, was not as unified nor as disciplined as before. Lastly and crucially, certain Christian leaders had evolved into a force for cunning and knavery, saying to themselves: Why should we give up what we have worked so hard to have, the respect of the empire and our piece of the pie? We have had quite enough of this crucifying the flesh, of being handed over to the mob, of having no hope for this life, of being hated by our families, of mourning while the world rejoices, of enduring violence for the faith. No, we have had our fill of suffering. It is not exactly true that we have become offended by the cross, its just that there are other ways of going about this rather than provoking the empire.

So the Christian leadership had been, to a great degree, seduced. They carried this seduction to its logical conclusion: Let us make peace with Rome, but we can still contend for the gospel by making it intellectual and academic, an argument among professors. By pursuing an endless rhetorical debate over the precise and absolute identity of Jesus, even to the most minute detail, they can shift the contention for the gospel to the mind, then pull away from the practice of actually being a Christian. This means that, for them, the hardest task has now been achieved, that Jesus of Nazareth now walks the halls of power in the person of the Emperor. So now Christian leaders can finally get some rest since all that needs to be done is to purify the doctrine, and once that is completed all this talk of suffering and confrontation with the world will just go away.

After the extinction of Paganism, the Christians in peace and piety might have enjoyed their solitary triumph. But the principle of discord was alive in their bosom, and they were more solicitous to explore the nature than to practice the laws of their founder. I have already observed that the disputes of the Trinity were succeeded by those of the Incarnation, alike scandalous to the church, alike pernicious to the state, still more minute in their origin, still more durable in their effects (p. 815 MLE).

This is what we have today, evangelical leaders being worthy successors to these hypocrites. Of course there have been exceptions, as in all generations, to this betrayal of Christianity. They are the remnant church, true heirs of the first Christians, but America's comfortable have sustained the hoax.

If Dobson and his fellow Lilliputian ministers want to argue that they have not made fools of the first Christians by their hypocrisy, let them. If they want to say they do not dress up the early Christians in Halloween costumes and parade them up and down main street, then I for one am perfectly willing to let them argue the point. Only please, dear reader, I beg you to let them deny, deny, deny all alone. Alone in their large sanctuaries, because it just costs too much in the way of time and spirit to have anyone there except their own echoes.

Some time ago we visited an evangelical Hispanic church in Colorado Springs. The pastor called up a boy who was leaving soon to fight in Iraq. In what could only be called a parody of New Testament commissioning, he prayed over him and blessed him in his efforts. I privately confronted the pastor afterwards, pointedly telling him that his blessing the sword was first a sin against Christ, then the boy, the congregation, and lastly the early church. His reply was that the early church had been split down the middle on the matter of Christians in the military. But he knew as well as I that the split did not begin in earnest until about 250 A.D., and those who pushed for military participation were a vocal minority. I angrily mentioned a few of the church fathers who absolutely forbid it, and this shepherd of the poor simply denied it. So, on the basis of what had occurred two and a half to three centuries after the life of Christ, and then only after compromise after compromise, the right reverend gives a young boy a spiritual pat on the back to either kill or be killed. And what will this do to the mind of Christ that is still young in him? In this case I blame myself first, for I should have pushed my way through the crowd to gently counsel this boy-soldier. Later, I could have addressed the priest, whom I suspected would talk nonsense about the early church and war.

It is a dark fact that priests and pastors like these have taken the place of ancient Rome as the oppressors of Christians around the world. The church of the persecuted has become the church of the persecutors. This oppression occurs more moderately in America but aggressively in poverty ridden nations. It is something of a Biblical miracle that in discussions with Christians in developing nations there is no bitterness expressed by the poor toward rich Christians, only they do want to be understood. One could liken it to the first church, a poor church, in Jerusalem reaching out for aid from her brethren around the empire. Unlike the church's answer then, pastoral authorities in the U.S. will not direct their congregations to send meaningful aid to the poor. For just as it is still true that stones do not weep, empire panderers will not engage in any mass rescue, having helped to make the poor poor in the first place. Take Jerusalem again: In one of the most remarkable ironies in religious history, evangelicals are sending their dollars not to hurting Christians in east Jerusalem, but to a political Israel that grows itself by taking the land of Palestinian Christians, just as Ahab did when he stole Naboth's land.

As with the poor church everywhere, Palestinian Christians have not called down fire, like James and John, upon an American church that lets a rebellious Israel do what it wishes. On the contrary, they ask for understanding and help in ending Israel's campaign against them. This ought to lead to remorse and character actions on the part of church leaders in the U.S. But it has not and likely will not. Thus a church father like Tertullian would have been justified, with James and John, in aiming his barbs at a well-pleased American clergy that will not utter a word of protest to a defiant Israel: 'You are fond of (megachurch) spectacles, expect the greatest of all spectacles, the last and eternal judgment of the universe.' Tertullian really ought to have stopped there, because what was needed eighteen hundred years ago is the same as what is needed now, transformation not divine justice.

Africans today do not take Tertullian as their example, though they would certainly have the right, humanly, to bring him to bear on their situation. What with the U.S.'s flabby episcopate bolstering politics as usual, thus no change for overwrought African churches, it is a New Testament miracle that those same churches do not express rage by excommunicating the whole lot of America's Mr./Ms. Popularity hungry clergy. Nor do they express pride against those who do them such harm. And again they would be in the right since there have been so many martyrs among them, far more than the early church.

In his defense of Christianity Tertullian, a North African, was correct in arguing that it was only on account of their religion that the Christians were jailed and executed by the Romans, and not for perjury, fraud, theft and robbery. But evangelicals are guilty of these at about the same rate as general society, and indeed in the criminal charge of hypocrisy its leaders far exceed that of general society. The early church's proximity to and protection of one another puts to eternal shame what these top authorities like to call the great blessing of a beautiful home in the suburbs. The first churches were, on the contrary, known for their thrift for the sake of the poor and distant churches, self-discipline as regards sexuality, eating and drinking as well as their refusal to take up arms and inactivity in larger matters of economy. This was seen as a real provocation in idolatrous Rome, for they chose professions and trades that were not 'careers,' but took on secondary importance to the local house church. They acted with integrity and honesty as they sought to protect their fragile reputation since they had to prove they were not a part of an unlawful conspiracy toward Rome, but were genuine and sincere. There were surrounded by a multitude of sects which sought the praise of the empire by the appearance of religion, and they had to show they were not one of them. The fruits of the spirit, which evangelicals speak endlessly of, were really fostered in their character by being so hated for their purity and simplicity. Persecutions drove them further underground but nearer together in mind, life and spirit. Of course they were victims, but they embraced their victimage as the suffering they had been commanded to endure, then considered what it would cost them if they were not so hated.

The primitive Christians never insisted that all Christians must be martyrs, nor do I. However, if evangelicals desire true Christianity then this option must be prayerfully sought out. Before any thought of martyrdom though, a certain character maturity must be reached. Paul himself was trained in Damascus for three years before beginning his ministry. So the local community of faith and the individual decide together whether martyrdom is an option. If it is determined that the individual is impetuous, or there is spiritual pride involved, then that option is taken off the plate for a time.

Evangelicals who have blindly trusted their leaders and

because of that have lived out a minimal approximation of Christianity, nearing their life's end, have a decision to make. They can appeal to grace, confessing they have been inexcusably lax with regard to the New Testament, the suffering of martyrdom of the first Christians and the current suffering of Christians in foreign lands. Or they can decide not to make this confession. Failing to confess, evangelicalism becomes nothing more than a late sleeper who, tardy for work, tries to sneak into his job as if nothing had happened, leaving it to his boss to decide what punishment is due the man who has .slept through his primary responsibility.

My Little Share of Authority

The presbyter Vigilantius, firmly, though ineffectually, withstood the superstition of the monks, relics, saints, fasts, etc. for which Jerome compares him to the Hydra, Cerberus, the Centaurs, etc. and considers him only as the organ of the Demon (Penguin p. 355).

I have never once said that I am a New Testament Christian, only that I am learning to become one, and there remains a wide gulf between it and me. If American pastors and priests want to contend they are more Christian than I am, then let them, and let Eternity decide the matter. But I hold a higher authority than they in two respects, in Socratic honesty and the Pauline. That I do not gloss over what the New Testament teaches (the pastors have, on the other hand, in front of their congregations, dedicated themselves to promulgating it), thus have not finessed the New Testament, but they did to pack their buildings. Of course my portrayal has not quite given me a promising career within the established American church. Yet I have freely chosen, voluntarily and as an adult, to live out certain crucial aspects of New Testament teaching, though it is equally true that I am really spineless, demonstrated by what I have left undone. This differs from middle class pastor/priests in four ways:

1) They will not admit and confess they are spineless
2) What they call Christian sacrifice, if any, was involuntary, a result of a difficult childhood etc.
3) They call suffering for the truth what the apostle Peter calls suffering for stupidity's sake, like tax audits on large properties, being mocked for opposing reasonable birth control or ridiculed for real hypocrisy etc.
4) They purposefully confuse the suffering that is common to secular society with Christian trials, such as raising children being called the cost of discipleship, being unable to pay their high mortgages a trial of faith, etc.

What I now say is boasting, I do not deny it, and may God forgive me for it. Yet I will take the risk and forge ahead with something I am compelled to do because of the condition that Christianity now finds itself in; rhetorical skill determines the cut of the Christian. While Dobson settles comfortably into a Colorado ski resort to write a new book (which evangelical readers await like the town band to provide background music to its arrival), I work a tent-making job (while Dobson collects a multi-million dollar settlement from Focus on the Family) in Eastern Europe, eking out a few minutes every day to try and get out another point of view. This while striving to save enough to give to the poor churches, personally and face-to-face, of the Middle East, Africa and India.

I am quite prepared to measure the New Testament

Christianity I have been led to pursue and for which I take no credit (like a wounded man on a horse that carries him home) against any middle class, media or megachurch pastor/priest in America. It boils down to who you are going to believe, which is of eternal concern for my reader. For if one chooses to follow a pastor whose whole life has been one long clever deception, then the reader will have died as he lived, a dupe who relied on his pastor's false authority. Then he will indeed have a poor excuse before the Eternal.

In my early twenties I recognized something was vitally wrong with the American church, though the thoughts were vague and inarticulate. In no way did I ever conceive of them as a revelation, but I knew I had to do something to balance the intellectual emphasis of the seminary with the Biblical reality of practicing one's faith, which in my case meant teaching in a low income neighborhood in east Los Angeles. There followed a course taught by a house church pastor where we looked at the New Testament demands of simplicity and a life lived within walking distance of each other. We knew these realities would help to drive out the two main idols within the American church, avarice (as seen through its holdings) and power (as seen by its silent and occasionally not so silent approval of evangelicals steering American politics). Then I saw my life's task standing before me, to make Christianity as clear as possible by exposing the crimes of a false church leadership and by first making the gospel apparent to myself. This I could do by striving to live it out among those whom Christ spent the majority of his time with, from the poor to the common man to the sincere.

One can then picture what the next few years would look like. House churches in Los Angeles, Denver, and D.C. Side jobs that often ended in a standoff over some ethical matter, detentions at nuclear trigger and military sites (for Christianly interfering in the U.S. sponsored massacres in Central America), preaching on the streets against the first Gulf War, war tax resistance, disputes at schools with mostly colleagues and administrators-this while living surrounded by those I spoke out for. It was Christianity on levels that the conformed church did not dare take on lest it completely abandon its mediocrity, but was very normal by New Testament standards. Here is how I viewed my effort: that of a man who chose a sometime loner's life therefore (if he loves the church) seeks to provide others the chance at living out the meaning of Christianity.

But the effort took its toll. It was coupled with two errors in judgment which forced me to rethink my choices. The first error was to misinterpret the NT doctrine of leadership and authority as democratic. This mistake in our house church led to yielding decision-making matters to the more outspoken, newer and more immature converts. The second error was presuming that fellow evangelicals would leap at the chance to be the church in the inner city, once they saw we were there to stay. Fear ended up keeping all but a few away. During this decade though I was, as now, particularly sensitive to my effort being checked by a proper humility, so that no profits or prestige should come my way. This I still am at pains to do. Nevertheless, I dared to believe, as now, I was becoming a New Testament Christian.

My conviction was that the more I shared the anguish of

the people in the neighborhood the more Christ would reveal what I was to do next: that by God's help my life was being structured to corral my worst tendencies. This structure served as preparation for something more demanding yet to come.

In 1991 the Gulf War began so a decade long companion and I sat down to decide an appropriate New Testament response. We were heartbroken yet incensed that our long time bosom friends and evangelical partners as well as the majority of the American churches were either going to keep silent or render up meaningless prayers of peace-without action. Then they would justify their indolence Christianly. Just like Vietnam. Thus it was in the spring of that year we decided, right or wrong, to shake the dust from our feet in order to have a lesser share of guilt in the complicity of the evangelical church. Though we were certain of our own share of that guilt, we ventured in faith and left America. Kent for Israel to assist peacemaking efforts and Palestinian laborers on a farm, and I for France to live in a village of largely special needs folk. We vowed to commit ourselves further in the works of faith, and to communicate often. This was the last time I would ever see him, for his journey was to come to an end three years later. He was run down on his bicycle close to the same village where my own journey had begun.

I can honestly say that since my departure from the U.S. more than two decades ago, that there was nothing in my personality that compelled me to leave. I could not understand how people could commit themselves to short term projects, like the Peace Corps, and certainly not the brief mission stints of most laity and clergy. But I did know this was to be a lifelong task, with no easy chair retirement home for missionaries at the end. I had bid a sad and angry farewell to a church leadership that had deserted the gospel. Yet I knew the battle against their mediocrity would be sustained on other fronts.

If I were to put down in writing the major events during this span, this minor effort would turn into a much larger one and there is something real doubtful about what the point would be. I can only bring out a few events here and there which do bear upon my point; that if evangelicals are to become Christian leaders then they must make the same effort the few have made, and continue to make, in order to be authentic New Testament shepherds.

The definition of Christian authority starts with going to the victim where he is. Then comprehending the situation better than the victim himself, if possible. If I do not attempt to experience it in the same way then I have nothing to say to him. I recall sitting in a cafe in west Jerusalem politely listening to an elderly American couple lecture on regional political/religious realities. I am rather deferential to the elderly so I did not say much. Yet they were quietly living in modern Jerusalem while I had to return to Palestinian Nablus (Shechem to Israelis), a city political Israel has turned into a poverty zone. So it was clear the couple were only looking for the respect that comes from living in Jerusalem, and that is not the same thing as the downward mobility that defines Christ nor Christian authority. Returning to Nablus I had to wait in line-like every other Palestinian-to cross through the checkpoint. In front of me was an old woman with her legs wrapped in bandages, being helped by her sons. After an hour's wait one of them turned to me and asked what I was doing there. I told him I taught English and volunteered with the church in Nablus. It was obvious I had no power over them, as the 19 year old sabra, or girl soldier did (along with the American government that pays her salary) but that I was there to help. I am in no way suggesting here that my suffering was as great as the Palestinians, yet this minimal attempt at understanding suffering as the victim understands it is the prerequisite to real Christian leadership. This stands in direct contrast to the pastor who takes his wealthier congregants on a tour or pilgimmage (as the Catholics call it) of the holy land. No, NT authority is to put up with the assumption that just like every other privileged foreigner you are there to take advantage of the victim. Thus, you are not willing to experience what they experience.

There have been hundreds of stories from my life abroad-blind village children in India, a furious Palestinian from a family uprooted by Israeli forces, Nigerians trapped in Belgrade during the war, lepers in unearthly beautiful gardens, Samaritans on their mountain, Guatemalan street children with cigarette burns on their arms courtesy of the police, former Polish solidarity workers made penniless by a lawless capitalism, a teenager maimed by torture in an Israeli prison, a hoard of beggars in Khartoum-it goes on. Adventurers could say the same so I dare not boast further. Yet what matters most is that if I did not humble myself and listen, I was not a Christian and washing no one's feet. There was one thing in all these encounters I knew to be of the highest importance, venturing to bring Christianity to bear on these conversations. This was the purpose of my being there, to understand as much as possible, capture interest, then provide the details that only the victim would know about. All to introduce a NT viewpoint. Whether it was laughing with the children at the animals on the street, a genuine and shared grief at the loss of a neighbor's child from malaria, a scarf dance among slum dwellers at a wedding etc. In each of these situations I admonish my reader to always remember, it is religious truth we were venturing to present. To do this inspite of our fear, for certainly the fear would fade and be replaced by boldness.

When in Palestine/Israel I often sit with Palestinian teens in their school canteens and listen as they claim they will take up arms against Israelis, with them knowing I too have been restricted in moving around due to the Israeli occupation. The teens are polite enough to wait for my response and I am all eagerness to give it: that they have not experienced enough of life yet to fire a rocket or even throw a rock against anyone. That there is another way they must explore, perhaps it is the Christianity a few of their nonviolent friends espouse. That as teens and students they owe themselves and God to investigate the religious options in life, and this they cannot do dying with a stone in their hand.

Bringing forward religious truth, this is the task of Christian authority. I am unspeakably honored to have as a friend an American in India, a companion of forty years. Of that time he has chosen to live sacrificially the past twenty six, and now other Christians there privately call him Saint John. John's life recalls Kierkegaard's words:

But in eternity it consoles him that he has suffered this, that he had exposed himself voluntarily to it, that he had not bolstered up his cause by any illusion, but with God-fearing shrewdness transmuted his sufferings into a treasure for eternity: the memory of sufferings endured, and of fidelity to himself and to his first love, beside whom he has loved only them that have suffered in this world . . . Yet it is true that he found also here on earth what he sought . . . It was the cause of Christianity he served, his life from childhood on being marvelously fitted for such a service . . . His purity of heart was to will only one thing. What his contemporaries complained of during his lifetime, that he would not abate the price, would not give in-this very thing is the eulogy pronounced upon him by after ages, that he did not abate the price, did not give in. But the grand enterprise he undertook . . . he could not ascribe to any man, least of all would he ascribe it to himself; if he were to ascribe it to anyone, it would be to Governance, to whom it was in fact ascribed, day after day and year after year . . . who historically died of a mortal disease, but poetically died of a longing for eternity, where uninterruptedly he would have nothing else to do but to thank God (The Point of View, Anthology pgs. 338-39).

This man would have been elected a bishop by the early church, an authority, empowered to discipline the apostate, heretic and wayward. Indeed, in the Indian city he lives in he is already a de facto authority. But not in America, not in the triumph of Rome, for when he returns to the U.S. he is just another odd but interesting storyteller on leave. On what roads of clerical depravity must he return? In one of the first churches he visits he is given five minutes to tell of his mission, whereas two young girls in miniskirts are given twenty to read flattering accounts of what their church means to them. He returns to songs of praise for Tammy Fae Baker, who just before her death complimented America's most notorious pornographic actor saying he was a fine young man (perhaps he would be a candidate for an ecclesial position?). He returns to hosannas of thanksgiving for Jerry Falwell, whose passing occasioned this eulogy by Franklin G Graham, that no matter their disagreements, whenever Falwell opened his Bible he was in agreement with him. He would say the same of his man Donald Trump. How praiseworthy and heartwarming they would all share the same Bible, a mix of selected verses from both Testaments. Let there be no misunderstanding, and I say this unequivocally and without apology, that not one American pulpit leader, whether it be Warren, Dobson, the Grahams, Jakes, Hagee, Robertson, Brewer, Meyers, Osteen, or any of the Reverend Tom, Dick, and Harrys, any media evangelist or talk show host, middle class or megachurch minister or priest is not Christianly worthy of tying John's shoes.

What we call pastor, priest, bishop, presbyter, minister, these reflect a level of prestige. Also a guaranteed income based on numbers, on how many can be attracted to their buildings. And in a nation where tens of millions call themselves evangelicals, no danger can in any way come from preaching Christ. Further, any pastor-if he is even a bit honest-will admit there is a certain dignity attached to it, as Rick Warren at the president's inaugeration might know.

I have said that we humans play rather loose with our

terminology, so that to say a New Testament leader and a contemporary evangelical leader are the same is as absurd as a town putting on a sparkler display and calling it war. If the American pastors want to call themselves Christian leaders then they must meet the job description laid out in 1 Timothy and the New Testament as a whole; if it is not their intention to be what the New Testament defines as Christian leaders, then they must not be identified as that. Call them what you will, 'evangelical leaders,' 'psychoanalytic therapists,' marriage and family counselors,' 'established church leaders,' 'pulpiteers,'there is a broad range of names at your disposal, except one. They are not to be called Christian leaders.

Over the past three decades I have confronted a bushel of these men and women-they are not hard to find-with their blasphemous use of this term and their sacreligious application of it to themselves. For whatever reason each has decided to carry on and cling to the term Christian leader, and so now about all that remains is their consciences. If there are any left. Make careful note then as to what the New Testament calls authorities. These men or women show no interest in government or war. They have exposed themselves to humiliation by rejecting the gods of the land, as well as the definition of holiness put forward by the cozy pastor/priests. They live simply, and are therefore prepared for every torment, first risking themselves then commissioning others (whom they know well) to follow their steps. Theirs is living with hair-trigger awareness that at any moment the people's resentment may flare up against them. Theirs is living with some verses embedded in their minds, such as there being a remnant left in Israel, all those who have not bowed the knee or kissed the feet of idols (money, politics, technology). It was refusals like this that led to the martyrdom of Bishop Cyprian [A.D. 258]:

Cyprianus should be immediately beheaded as the enemy of the gods of Rome, and as the chief and ringleader of a criminal association which he had seduced into an impious resistance against the laws of the most holy emperors, Valerian and Gallienus (p. 298 MLE).

The crime? The refusal to sacrifice to Roman gods.

Now the evangelical elite would never find themselves in Cyprian's shoes, having delivered up coliseums full of sacrifices to their government over the years, the most criminal being young Christians sent to war to lose either their lives or their Christianity. But know, my reader, know that the stories of the old martyrs will find their way into the sermons of its ecclesiastics. Know that their cheeks will glisten with the tears they will shed because the circumstances do not reveal themselves to be the martyrs that they really are.

And why will the circumstances not allow America's pastors to shine as martyrs? Because in the American evangelical church there is nothing to persecute. Nothing. Does the darkness persecute darkness when it sees it in the church?

I have little doubt that inspite of everything in the New Testament, evangelical authorities, especially in the megachurches, will stick to being called Christian authorities. If pastors on the middle-class-on-up spectrum have any desire not to be made into laughingstocks-particularly by the young-they will plead with their bishops not to apply this term to themselves or their colleagues. Doing so would only take their clownishness to the second power.

I do not hesitate to mention here that I have met some sincere pastors in the U.S., but many more in countries where it is dangerous to be a Christian leader. None of them call themselves Christian leaders. Yet they fully meet the criteria. But I have not met one American pastor from the middle-class-on-up category that is not the early church's idea of a monstrous farce.

Of course it would be a step in the right direction if evangelical ringleaders would (fingers glued to their pulpits, sweating profusely) admit publicly they have not been Christian leaders. On the contrary, religious representatives of conformed religion.

I harbor no illusion that this will occur on any widespread scale. What is most crucial is that the case has been made and the choice is clear. I can already hear the charge being laid against me by the most zealous defenders of their ministers. 'You are demanding all or nothing!' No, I have never said that. What I am calling for is a little transparency that admits that the pastor/priests are not Christian authorities. Better to come right out with it and confess they are worldly religious guides and glad of it.

My sense is that everything will go on as usual. That, as in politics, everything-in-moderation, there-has-to-be-some-middle-ground, don't-fix-it-if-its-not-broken form of church leadership will prevail for a long time. No matter how nauseatingly rotten that church leadership is. But if you my reader dare to accept the godly ambition of some day being a Christian leader according to New Testament protocol, but go ahead anyway and take the broad road the contemporary church points out to you, you end with no Christian authority. Further, you risk perdition. No, your credibility as a true pastor lies in actions which are most repugnant to your normal inclinations: power, prestige, and financial security. Though family and the majority of your friends earnestly beseech you, though your pastor publicly commends you (then promptly ignores you), patronizingly smiling down on Monday what he praised on Sunday, nothing will deprive you of that crown of glory. It comes from living out the narrative of Luke, speaking the truth while living among the poor. This makes you a Christian authority, for this service links you to Christ. By this you are made ready with Him to judge the entire creation. This indeed is an exalted desire, but it can only come through humiliation.

Your siding with the poor (or your honesty if you have not), will have a blinding effect. Like the sun shining off the shields of the Hebrews against the opposing army, upon those whom you thought were Christians and thus were with you. Unwilling to see clearly they attribute your actions and honesty to pride or naivete. So the more you plunge into act and being the more conformed they become. You feel abandoned and betrayed, and so you are. Then comes the word of consolation from over three thousand autumns ago: 'The Lord will provide . . .'

Fourth Century Roman Christendom and the Contemporary Worldly Church

Prosperity had relaxed the nerves of discipline. Fraud, envy, and malice prevailed in every congregation. The presbyters aspired to the episcopal office, which every day became an object more worthy of their ambition. The bishops, who contended with each other for ecclesiastical preeminence, appeared by their conduct to claim a secular and tyrannical power in the church (p. 303-04 MLE).

American Christendom would have been the inveterate enemy of the early Christians, then later the pandering friend of nearly all the fourth century Caesars. Here is why:

When pagan Rome first looked down upon the early church, they were accused of 'atheism and Jewish manners.' Some magistrates allowed the mob and pagan priests to act upon their consuming hatred for the transgressors of their ancestor's religion. The Caesars grew increasingly offended and began to deliver them up to persecutions. Yet in one thing Rome was correct, they at least recognized Christianity for what it was. But the polytheists, having given up the attempt to rid Rome of the new religion, elected to wait this upstart faith out. Too, with a bit of sugar here and an apple there, coax the wild horse into a trap. Thus in the course of three centuries Christianity went from being:

The defense of [their] persons and property they knew not how to reconcile with the patient doctrine which enjoined an unlimited forgiveness for past injuries and commanded them to invite the repitition of fresh insults. Their simplicity was offended by the use of oaths, by the pomp of magistry, and by the active contention of public life; nor could their humane ignorance be convinced that it was lawful on any occasion to shed the blood of [their] fellow-creatures, either by the sword of justice, or by that of war; even though their criminal or hostile attempts should threaten the peace and safety of the whole community . . . The Christians felt that [government] institutions might be necessary for the present system of the world, and they cheerfully submitted to the authority of their Pagan governors. But while they inculcated the maxims of passive obedience, they refused to take any active part in the civil administration or the military defense of the empire . . . it was impossible that the Christians, without renouncing a more sacred duty, could assume the character of soldiers, of magistrates, or of princes (p. 259 MLE) (italics mine).

Three hundred years later, Christianity had become this:

A great number of the soldiers had already consecrated their sword to the service of Christ and of Constantine. The habits of mankind and the interests of religion gradually abated the horror of war and bloodshed which had so long prevailed among the Christians; and in the councils which were assembled under the gracious protection of Constantine, the authority of the bishops were seasonably employed to ratify the obligation of the military oath, and to inflict the penalty of excommunication on those soldiers who threw away their arms during the peace of the church (p. 383-84 MLE).

Gibbon notes the Empire's executioners were largely a cowardly group of grasping and ambitious clergy eager to advance up the ecclesiastical ladder by blessing Caesar's Christianity. America's own spiritless group of clerical parasites just cannot stop heaping praise of their own, as we note from Graham and Nixon's carpet bombing in Vietnam, Dobson and Bush's Iraq, Warren and Obama's drone terrorism etc. One wonders how far the pastor/priests will go, having already constructed a hundred thousand large edifices and called them churches, become master rhetoricians and called this preaching, become shrewd media and marketing wizards and called this advancing the gospel. Could it get any worse than this?

The precedent was set by the indolence, prosperity, and cowardice of the majority of fourth century church leadership. They had conveniently forgotten that the persecution of the first three centuries had produced a healthy, vigorous, militant church alive to the odds it was facing, knowing it had divine protection. The more intense the heat of hatred, the greater the integrity and quality of the church. But in America's leaderless wasteland, there is nothing to persecute. Nothing. Would the public suddenly decide to go on the offensive against its own best and brightest servants, its church leadership? No, they would and will not. And why would the public do this, for the secure clergy gives them no reason. Why would the Right Reverend give up an ounce of his prestige, a sliver of his enjoyment of life? Would the public suddenly imprison the pastor/priests on the charge of complicity to enjoy the pleasures of the American way of life?

Whether evangelical leaders are conscious of this or not is irrelevant. It is heresy in practice by which they are by no means the first. They carry on a long tradition beginning with the priests, monks and theologians who made an accord with Rome, where they had mediated and compromised Christendom into becoming the sparkling light of the Empire. The cathedral churches became massive. Soldiers slaughtered in the name of Christ. Prosperity was profuse.

Outside of Rome-similar to America-the capitulation of the church did not entirely take hold. Right in the middle of all that worldliness in the fourth century were the Syrian and Egyptian churches, raising a cry of defiance:

'The Testament of our Lord,' which forbids a soldier to be baptized unless he leaves the service, and forbids a Christian to become a soldier on pain of excommunication, was compiled in Syria or southeastern Asia Minor not earlier than the middle of the fourth century. The Egyptian Church-Order, which lays down the same ruling, with the modification that, if a soldier has been received into membership and is commanded to kill, he is not to do it, and if he does he is to be rejected, is usually thought to belong to the first half of the fourth century . . . The existence of these Church-Orders is conclusive proof that in large sections of the Christian community, the decision(s) taken by official Christendom . . . were not accepted (Cadoux, The Early Christian Attitude to War, p. 259-60).

Even in Rome there was resistance, for the first three hundred years of the church's life had not been forgotten in one generation:

The decision(s) [about war] to which the leaders and the majority of the church were committed by the patronage of Constantinus were very far from winning the immediate and unanimous assent of Christendom . . . the popularity of the Emperor Julianus (361-363 A.D.) with the army and the support it gave him in his reversion to Paganism presuppose a comparatively small proportion of Christians in it (Cadoux p. 260-61).

The buffoonery of the court flatterers now was vaulted into prominence by the compromises made then:

The consequence was that when the triumph of Constantinus suddenly called upon the Church to come down definately on one side of the fence or the other, she found that a free decision was no longer open to her. Her joy at the deliverance Constantinus had wrought for her was so great that it put her off her guard . . . Henceforth it was out of the question for her to insist on an ethical view and practice, on which her own mind was not completely made up, and which [Constantinus] would inevitably regard as dangerous disloyalty to himself (Cadoux, p. 262).

Pagan Rome, which hungered after Greek philosophy as a calf seeks its mother's milk, had generally made hedonism and its religious counterpart, Epicureanism, its model. So the early church took it on in hand-to-hand spiritual combat through voluntary poverty, austerity, self-denial and martyrdom. But by the fifth century the Christians had become so brutal, ethically, that it was normal practice to be upright personally yet socially cruel, a characteristic of modern evangelicalism (with regard to global poverty, war, climate, and torture). Augustine supplies us with proof:

> *In the field of battle, in partial encounters, in single combats, he [Count Boniface] was still the terror of the Barbarians: the clergy, and particularly his friend Augustine, were edified [by] . . . his spotless integrity; the army dreaded his equal and inexorable justice, which may be displayed in a very singular example. A peasant who complained of the criminal intimacy between his wife and a Gothic soldier was directed to attend his tribunal the following day: in the evening the count . . . rode ten miles into the country, surprised the guilty couple, punished the soldier with instant death, and silenced the complaints of the husband by presenting him . . . with the head of the adulterer (p. 595 MLE).*

Out of Augustine's friendship with Boniface sprang the notion of the Just-therefore good-War, which Augustine said was divinely inspired. This gave eternal sanction to Christian killing, though it left the church entirely without substance.

In a similar movement some sixteen hundred years later we look at what has now become a constant effort of the worldly church to place one of their own in positions of political and military power. We doubt that fourth century Christians could have shouted louder hallelujahs when Theodosius ascended the throne than when the younger Bush did. Theodosius would have met all the contemporary criteria for a successful political career:

> *Theodosius was the first of the emperors baptized in the true faith of the Trinity [February 28, A.D. 380] . . . and as the emperor ascended from the holy font, still glowing with the warm feelings of regeneration, he dictated a solemn edict, which proclaimed his own faith and prescribed the religion of his subjects [Catholic Christianity] (p. 512 MLE).*

And what was the character of the church leadership during his reign?:

> *In an age when the ecclesiastics had scandalously degenerated from the model of apostolic purity, the most worthless and corrupt were always the most eager to frequent, and disturb, the episcopal assemblies. The conflict and fermentation of so many opposite interests and tempers inflamed the passion of the bishops: and their ruling passions were the love of gold and the love of dispute (p. 515 MLE).*

And what did this heavenly example inspire in the general populace?

> *A long period of calamity or decay must have checked the industry and diminished the wealth of the people; and their profuse luxury must have been the result of that indolent despair which enjoys the present hour and declines the thoughts of futurity . . . And the mad prodigality which prevails in the confusion of a shipwreck or a seige may serve to explain the progress of luxury amidst the misfortunes and terrors of a sinking nation (p. 520 MLE).*

It must not startle the reader then that polls have shown evangelicals to be more inclined to torture than secular society. Again Theodosius sets the precedent:

The influence which Ambrose [bishop of Milan] and his brethren had acquired over the youth of [emperor] Gratian and the piety of Theodosius was employed to infuse the maxims of persecution into the breasts of the Imperial proselytes . . . (p. 522 MLE) (italics mine).

Alas, modern evangelical pulpiteers never entered into the debate over such actions. Any serious dispute regarding evangelicals assimilating the cruelty of secular politics in America has not existed for a long time. By primitive church norms the American church today is largely fitness, flabbiness, and practical heresy. Layers and layers of yellow fat brought on by sitting down and thinking politics, mammon, gadgets, electronics, cars, luxury-along with inexperienced, terrified, hat-in-hand religious writers all of which has brought us right back to fourth century Rome/Constantinople. Christianity was meant to battle tooth and nail with the world, not willing to pay a penny to make common cause. The court flatterers now glide through all handshakes and smiles while sparring on an issue here and there (abortion, contraception, family, gay marriage, creation, sexual integrity, etc.), when it might pave their way pleasurably through their four score and ten.

American pastorate, behold Rome.

Ecclesia Abhorrere Sanguis: The Church Shrinks from Bloodshed?

He [Clovis] exclaimed with indiscreet fury, 'Had I been present at the head of my valiant Franks, I would have revenged his [Christ's] injuries' . . He was still more incapable of feeling the mild influence of the gospel which persuades and purifies the heart of a genuine convert. His ambitious reign was a perpetual violation of moral and Christian duties: his hands were stained with blood in peace as well as in war . . . (pgs. 662-63 MLE) (italics mine).

If by recalling this saying of the first church, that the church shrinks from bloodshed, my intention was to teach the pastorate New Testament truth, then certainly Dobson (who might be too busy hunting bears to take notice) and company will say I am so far out of touch with what born-again means that nothing I say can be trusted. For evangelical leaders have definitely not been shrinking lately, but have yielded splendid results in their support of presidential war campaigns.

Given that every one of the major religions (Koranic Islam only at times) takes the option of peace seriously and that this is one crucial way one pursues truth, and given that this is so hard because the human yearning for vengeance is so strong, thus the more effort one puts into peacemaking the harder it becomes. For church guides have learned well from their history about what to do with the troublesome term of peacemaking. It is a cunning maneuver to feint in one direction so as to score in another, and this our comfortably fit/flabby guides are eager to learn. The trick is this: to step-by-step psychologically alter the term peacemaking to peaceloving so that one's Christian obedience, the obedience of being a Christian slowly drops away. Then once that Pandora's box is opened, church leaders can lay back in their easy chairs. Now their lives are made even more comfortable-more family time, golf, flat screen TVs-because now we have become that blessed, fortunate, peaceloving nation. All one need do to maintain it is to vote the prolife ticket, support the Dobson and Perkins version of family, and say that one loves peace and that will be enough to fulfill the commandment to be a peacemaker.

Better still, make all evangelicals into the likes of Osteen, Jakes, the Grahams, Wilkerson, LaHaye, Copeland, Hinn, Warren, et al, whose well known love for God is spread daily with the help of money and the media, but whose actual lives have nothing at all to do with the gospel of peace. Then you can really take in the best America has to offer, from well-appointed homes to Hawaiian vacations, along with the guarantee that things will get better still. No need to actually travel to the Green Line (the divide between Israel and Palestine), to stand between the combatants, that is for diplomacy to resolve. No evangelical leader in his right mind would seriously even consider going to a nuclear weapons plant to get on his knees and pray that the diabolical thing (a swords into ploughshares prayer) gets dismantled, for America is the defender of the Good and Christianity. Further, no pastor/priest should ever command a Christian to lay down his weapons (inspite of Christ's command to Peter to do just that), for war is justified in the Old Testament for the nation that follows the Lord. For capital crimes bring in the executioner, for the law of Exodus is more important than Christ's command not to kill/murder. Never forbid the possession of a gun by believers, for those guns are the real peacemakers. Rewrite then with your life the very foundation, heart, and root of what the Divine, what Christ's view of reality is; it shows progress by how much more comfortable church leaders are. For this they can thank God himself (it just means that the New Testament is a lying thief of their comfort) that their conversations flow more smoothly and they can share a few burdens over a fine dinner. Yes, this is the way to go, their way is eased, upward mobility is accelerated and America is for them that altogether blessed land of the exceptional, with the prospects even better for their children. Only they must avoid peacemaking, and its as if a thousand butterflies have been set free; they finally have enough time to advance their careers, which can be done in the name of Christ. Believe the pastor/priest when they say they are only teaching how to be in the world and not of it. For all Christians do this, thus the pastor is waiting to offer recognition, recognition for cunning. It is the same recognition that all those other Christians receive, because when they recognize others they are really just congratulating themselves. They have indeed reached a special understanding with both God and their congregations/parishes. Whether this understanding with God really exists is a matter that will be taken up when the pastor/priest meets Governance.

So it is with the compromised church. When the New Testament commands peace (peace on earth), when the Old Testament strongly hints at it, at times commands it (love your neighbor as yourself), when there are abundant examples of it (Job, Joseph, Elisha and the Arameans), evangelical leaders simply run away and hide behind slogans and phrases. Their favorite: that it is in 'the heart,' and in 'the heart alone' that there is peace. Now this phrase puts a premium on peaceloving, which acts like a sedative, and that is a grotesque pastoral shrewdness that alters the meaning of peacemaking. For Biblically peace is not just in the heart, but it is divisive, inflaming! Here the soothing preacher of peace in the heart makes his case: 'What God desires is obedience to Government, to render to Caesar. To do otherwise is to be a radical, a communist, heretical, well-meaning perhaps but misguided, disobedient to the Lord; change your ways. God does not want you to be a disturber of a government He Himself has ordained; concentrate on only your personal relationship with the Lord and you will be like the many who have come to know real peace in their hearts, a peace that passes understanding'-which is to say: be peaceloving, maintain peaceful interpersonal relations, cast good wishes about as you would flowers before the bridal pair, ignore the bloodshed brought on by business/politics and then join us in our trembling before God for having made such choices:

In the age of the crusades, the Christians both of the East and the West, were persuaded [to go to war]. their arguments are clouded by the perpetual abuse of Scripture and rhetoric [and preaching]; but they seem to insist on the impiety of their Pagan and Mohammedan foes (p. 1051 MLE) (italics mine).

When one man, one woman, cannot be sedated by this kind of eternal assurance, he will be accused of exaggeration, of going beyond what the Bible itself says, of seeking attention, and in the case of the Catholics directed to the monastery. Church leaders, with a characteristic lack of passion, will simply remove him from leadership. The young Sunday School teacher, a Timothy, a Priscilla, who tells the eight year olds that Christianity forbids they become soldiers, will meet with parental hatred; this is exactly what the New Testament says will happen to the Christian, though it could hardly predict how spiritless that leadership would become. In any event, clergy playing at Christianity will do the necessary dismissals, the same clergy who have been baptized and ordained in the name of Christ.

What will this clergy get in return for not shrinking from bloodshed? When clerics are silent about or take a share in the sword, when they rid themselves of the one who so annoyingly keeps repeating New Testament truths, when they walk away from the discussion, then a measure of everlasting justice will be meted out according to their blood-guilt. For they chose to listen to their colleagues and the masses, rather than the New Testament:

In the quarrels of ancient Greece, the holy people of Elis enjoyed a perpetual peace under the protection of Jupiter and in the exercise of the Olympic games. Happy would it have been if a similar privilege had guarded the patrimony of St. Peter from the calamities of war; if the Christians . . . would have sheathed their swords . . . (p. 878 MLE).

Why Colorado Springs, Being the Nerve Center for Evangelical Leadership, is the City Furthest from God on Earth

The pastoral labors of the archbishop of Constantinople provoked, and gradually united against him, two sorts of enemies [A.D. 398-403]; the aspiring clergy . . . and the obstinate sinners, who were offended by his reproofs. When Chrysostom thundered from the pulpit of St. Sophia against the degeneracy of the Christians, his shafts were spent among the crowd without wounding or even marking the character of any individual. When he declaimed against the peculiar vices of the rich . . . the guilty were still sheltered by their numbers . . . (p. 583 MLE).

The crux of the matter: Portraying Colorado Springs, because of the many prominent evangelical organizations, as a Christian city, Christian of the first order based on the New Testament.

Be assured every conceivable means will be used to confuse this issue, to throw a thousand interpretations on it, to bury the matter in questions, to mask it through scholarly interviews etc. The newspapers, principally the Springs' own Gazette-as well as the Independent, which sees the issue as irrelevant-will lead the way in muddle-headed diversion. Evangelical media wings will only pay attention to the matter if it becomes public, just as most organizations. But if they do decide, in their infinite wisdom, that the issue of Colorado Springs being an alleged Christian city is important, then know that they will turn the thing into a hydra of confusion and distraction.

The genuine Christian will not budge from his premise: It is all too clear that the high-salaried and materially refined clerics, by yoking themselves to America, have correspondingly descended into the darkest depths of a betrayal of Christianity.

If we accept the premise that the Springs is a Christian city, we must accept that every city in India is a Christian city. The general population there accepts Christ into its pantheon of gods (as evangelical leaders accept Him alongside their pantheon of politics, prestige, purse, military firepower, technology, etc). Indian cities are also opposed to gay marriage, its patrons faithful to their spouses, have strong families (with few family planning clinics) and many are opposed to abortion. They uphold the law and pay their taxes. Thus most cities, towns, and villages around the globe could make just as strong a claim of being Christian and often do.

When it comes to this slight matter of the Son of Man having to suffer, then daring to demand the very same thing from His followers ('I am the way,' 'Do as I have done for you,' 'Follow me,' 'His sheep follow Him,'), it means less than nothing to these well-groomed shepherds. For they accept Him as the Redeemer and shun Him as the Pattern. Or, in an absolute mockery of Christian suffering, mix the pain that is common to all humankind (accidents, mortgage defaults, bankruptcy, layoffs, etc.) with the cross of Christ. Bearing the cross of Christ means to suffer for the truth, and the leadership lumps it all together with everyday aches in a kind of stone soup.

The Springs marches on, as oblivious to the actual life of Jesus Christ as tame geese, who, alerted to the presence of the hunter, continue to waddle passively.

Colorado Springs, second in the nation-to Las Vegas-in suicides, what a massive eternal accounting awaits your evangelical shepherds. For they have linked themselves with Christianity, thus making the Springs out to be 'This Beautiful City' for Christianity. Where Wheaton once was, they now stand. Yet the more the honest man confronts the truth the more he sees that the Springs replaced secularism with hypocrisy, honesty with Christendom. The whole terrific number of the city's well off priests/pastors would do better to head up Pike's Peak and there curse God, find new ways to laugh at Him, and compete in a sarcasm contest aimed at His goodness. They would all gather there and each carve out, in stone, a new Ten Commandments. Then they would hold it up before God and tell him what He forgot, that what He lacked they would make up for in patriotism and numbers.

Young people, far be it from you to lack enthusiasm for the faith; you who plunge headlong into projects to assist your neighbor, who yearn with all passion for the Truth to be preached to the ends of the earth. In your maturity leave the theatrical suburbs behind and shake every blade of manicured lawn from your feet and head not only for summer projects but for a life

immersed in faith, being despised and misunderstood, risking
bodily harm or, Lord forbid, madness and suicide. Do this and
you are redeemed. You cannot redeem all the scribes/pharisees/
pastors/priests of a city like Colorado Springs, for on a human
level their crimes against humanity are nearly irredeemable yet
you, you, can be delivered.

The situation is like a city that sought to be the Paris of the
American west, a city of art and intellect, but as yet has failed to
secure one art museum, where public debate was banned and
outdoor cafes were seen as eyesores. Since the city's brochures
declared itself a Paris, would the rest of the world agree? Would
it not make more sense for the city to say 'We are no Paris,' so as
to avoid becoming a laughingstock?

There is no argument: The city of Colorado Springs has
made God out to be a blithering idiot. One of the most financially
comfortable cities in the world has earned money by claiming
that it is a hub for Christianity; one hundred organizations and
its Gazette declaring that its main aim in life is the spread of
Christianity just as it slithers through a maze of New Testament
obstacles. You would think that the city's government would
keep quiet about this, suffer its shame in silence, ask how they
got themselves into this and address the matter. What was it that
attracted this horde of widow robbers and further, what can be
done about it. But no, no, such a thing is unheard of in major
cities. Their goal was to attract business not drive it away. A lot
of revenue and influence was involved so they lowered taxes and
land values for evangelical corporations. Lo and behold Focus
on the Family had its multi-million dollar campus, next to to a

Hilton Hotel, on the cheap and now a good time will be had by all. True, this sort of attitude is to be expected of unbelieving city officials.

But when the whimpering orators defend the city as a Christian city, a center for moral values, then we have another matter. Every day in the chapel services of these evangelical corporations Christ's name is called upon (so He is there) with the plea that the Springs become even more a Christian city. Odd that the New Testament is not taken into account, where the first church members lived simply, were spit on, abandoned, misunderstood, taken to court, and scoffed at. No, those who defend the Springs as Christian have their own idea of a city of Christ: it is perpetually the recipient of financial/military favors, conservative accolades and visits, media coverage, national applause, a pattern for cities across the nation, a bastion of moral values. This unique understanding of a Christian city is how they interpret words like 'continue to live in Him' from Colossians 2:6. This verse at one time defined the Christian life as denying oneself, as abandoning a life of pleasure for the cause of Christ, to cling to Christian conscience, to not brood over what could have been, but to the very last breath, possibly a blood witness' final whisper, fight the good fight. The time when 'continue to live in Him' was thus understood is now gone. The Springs' top clerics take these words to mean something else, to be proud the city is a moral guide, just look at all the effort it took to become one: see that you are like James Dobson, not Christ, who says forebodingly 'Woe to you who are rich.'

How did the Springs come to, under the banner of

Christendom, amass its material wealth? One way was simply
to mow down and bludgeon others into handing it over. While
in the U.S. my side job was to assist special needs children in
schools around the Springs, which means on my way to work
I had to pass the Crusader castles, the vicious triangle: the
largely evangelical maker of killer weapons, Lockheed Martin,
then Dobson's luxurious Focus building, often ending up at the
Air Force Academy. There stand two large pagan gods, one a
jet fighter the other a bomber, both carrying the blood guilt
of a few million Vietnamese, Iraquis, Afganis etc. along with
countless numbers of special needs children. Next to the gods
is the architectual wonder of the Academy, a gleaming white
triangular shaped chapel. My suggestion is to turn the chapel
into a discotheque-an ethical advance compared to its current
use, calling upon Christ so in their hypocrisy the chaplains can
dress Him up as an ape.

What use to write the Spring's Gazette or the Denver Post
who have demonstrated their abiding concern for truth and the
common man. What use to confront the pastors, priests and
chaplains whom I know from personal experience feign like
they do not know what I am talking about. I will be content
with using my pen and my voice from time to time, and if I am
dismissed as a ranter then I can find consolation in the Author
of the New Testament, and those who are out there on the front
lines, along with my own soul, which has a decent grasp of
things too.

It is enough to announce that this mecca for evangelical
leaders is not a Christian city, then to say it succinctly and clearly

wherever it is implied that it is. Would that Christians around the world take offence and ratchet up their protest to the level this blasphemous nonsense has already reached, of the Springs being a center for born again Christians, a place of positive spiritual growth and a pillar of true religion. For more than two decades, since Haggard's vision on the side of Pike's Peak, the city's church heads have cast a magic spell over their audience, in this case an entire city was entranced. This does not look good to outsiders, except when they are too fascinated with the show.

That Pastor Haggard and New Life Church were Warned, Repeatedly, before his downfall

The gates of reconciliation and Heaven were seldom shut against the returning penitent; but a severe and solemn form of discipline was instituted, which, while it served to expiate his crime, might powerfully deter the spectators from the imitation of his example . . . If the fault was of a very heinous nature, whole years of penance were esteemed an inadequate satisfaction to the Divine Justice; and it was always by slow and painful gradations that the sinner, the heretic, or the apostate, was readmitted into the bosom of the church (Penguin p. 170-171).

Upon my return to the U.S. every autumn I had noted the growing membership rolls of Pastor Haggard's New Life congregation (I had come from third world house churches). I had watched this man shoot to the top of his profession (Christianly to move upwards is to suffer greater persecution), listening to him speak of his oft-made trips to Washington, being on Bush's 'speed dial,' preaching in a palace decorated with the flags of nations (a million hungry children around the world are now in their graves because of this white-washed tomb). At a young age he had been appointed to the presidency of a 30 million member evangelical association (when Christians are told they will be a remnant and a little flock), a bright and rising star (see the New Testament on receiving honor from men) who was beginning to appreciate the fruit of his labors: a fabulous income, the esteem of suburban evangelicals, the satisfaction of being a mover and shaker on a global scale. One can certainly understand why Pastor Haggard would not want to admit that his type of Christianity is as different from the New Testament as a vulture is from a dove, much less let go of it for the sake of the truth:

By their [the pastors/priests] contempt of the world, they insensibly acquired its most desirable advantages . . . The delicate plenty of an opulent household . . . The immense fortunes of the Roman ladies were gradually consumed . . . [he] presumed to declare, with the smooth face of hypocrisy, that he was the only instrument of charity and the steward of the poor. The lucrative but disgraceful trade which was exercised by the clergy to defraud . . . (p. 479 MLE) (italics mine).

His actions though did not result in my inactivity or resignation. No indeed, for this purpose I have been bred since my mid-twenties, when I rejected ordination and all that accompanies it: salaries, robes, appellations, the regard of the community etc., things which by New Testament standards are dubious. It was from this standpoint that I first approached Haggard, knowing that his prior ordination meant that he had either taken an oath upon the New Testament or had been confirmed in its teaching. The ordination and teaching were, in themselves, warnings to him. But being aware of Old

Testament warnings that were directed TO ME if I were to do nothing, spoke out against his kind of Christianity in front of their meeting center, and was quickly removed from the area by Security (the temple guards). As I was being led away I was told to 'make an appointment' with the good pastor to 'discuss my concerns.' Not desiring to humor His Honor, needing only to utter a few words of warning, I waited until he was done with his performance one Sunday morning then stood in line behind those waiting to shake his hand and sing his praises. When my turn came I briefly introduced myself, said a bit about our mission work, and told him Christ's own words, that he sell the building, give the money to the poor, and follow Him. I let him know he needed to be taught and instructed, perhaps by us in India. Haggard, not expecting this, quickly recovered his suburban civility, stuck out his hand and thanked me for my opinion. Prepared for this, I witheld my hand (thus my peace) and told him why I was withholding that peace. He had had enough of me by then and turned back to the praises.

The last confrontation had to be public and before the church (there is an orderly process for this in Matthew). Since I had already been removed once from their castle campus I chose to wait for a more opportune time. It came when he was doing a booksigning for his most recent masterpiece. At the bookstore I indicated, somewhat loudly, to the milling crowd that the pastor was a fraud and a hypocrite. Just before I was threatened with police action by an associate pastor, I caught a glimpse of Haggard suddenly quite taken with autographing the book in front of him, a nervous smile on his lips. I had just rung another alarm, and had been regarded as nothing more than a ranter.

Neither I nor New Life church were in any way aware at the time of his sexual liasons. I did not learn of them until I returned from India a couple years later. I knew immediately that, just as in the case of the priest's sex scandals, the much greater sin lies in his worldly conformity. That the accompanying scandal was God's way of calling the church's attention to his being merely another soft-clothed orator, entirely spiritless.

Now of course there is more hope for Haggard, if he should relinquish playing Christianity and turn toward remorse/confession/repentence. The quality of the redemption must correspond with the enormity of the offence (for he who has been forgiven much, loves much). The offence(s) of profound hypocrisy against Christianity must not be compounded by reintegrating himself into another pastoral position in an upper middle class church. Since he has done just this, taken on yet another clerical post, one must wonder whose spiritual condition is worse, Haggard's or his successor at New Life, Brady Boyd (who was personally handed a copy of this work), or any of the other evangelical nincompoops who shape the conformed church. For Haggard God's ax has only partially fallen, and he has ignored it. The fact that he faced global humiliation though should be enough to bring fear and trembling upon any ego that attempts to apply (by hypocrisy and lies) cosmetics to God's face. There is a greater horror still, a horror so horrible it cannot be thought, and that is God's withholding of an even greater earthly judgment than Haggard experienced. And why is it being withheld? So that the pastor's worldliness is spread out over an entire lifetime. It is allowed to accumulate because of the heinousness of the crimes (not the least being deceiving others into believing that what they have before them is a real man of God). Then, when all is revealed, they will see that those warnings were really not to be trifled with.

Church-going family man, eager and earnest to maintain the integrity of your marriage and raise your children up in the fear of the Lord, did you not puzzle at Pastor Haggard more than once; were you not occasionally lost in silent thought as you viewed his spectacular theater displays (now duplicated by Boyd) and compared it to the reality of a life that was in fact lived in agony and culminated with curses, scourging and crucifixion? Did it not perhaps once cross your mind that there was a distance the length of eternity between Haggard's living well off his preaching and the honest-to-goodness horror of the real thing?

Now that Haggard has returned to the conformed church may it not be held against me if secular society should gain regular amusement by his preaching (are you not entertained?), for even if it does not understand what regular preaching is, it is attuned to a bit of religious comedy, of which most ministers (even more than politicians) seem ever so willing to provide. Then they claim their being mocked is suffering for Christ, which is even more entertaining etc.

The last time I saw Haggard was in a Mexican restaurant-an accidental meeting. He was speaking with a couple of men, who appeared rapt with attention. Knowing this man had been responsible for the starvation and death by illness of perhaps a million children, I would never forgive myself if I let him eat his meal in peace. I calmly interrupted them and warned the two men not to heed this deceiver. Then I asked, after identifying myself again as a missionary, if I could explain myself. One of them stood up to confront me (which I took as a no), so I began walking out, followed by Haggard's slew of curses and threats of eternal damnation, delivered by the former president (on behalf of?) of the American Association of Evangelicals, to which I did not respond.

What is done is done now and I have nothing more to say to Haggard, for I am confirmed of his desperate need for the applause of, if not millions, certainly thousands. His very public life now has allowed me to show what he, Boyd and friends are really after: (1) that they are pastors only in the sense of shepherding popularity, photos, splendid salaries, and interviews toward themselves; (2) that they skip over, ignore, shove aside, and blunt anything that has to do with the pivotal matters of imitating Christ's life; (3) what pleasant security the suburban family may dwell in on this issue of everlasting life by trusting such court flatterers.

What makes me think I was successful in attaining my aim (and I knew from the outset Haggard would in no way challenge my statements, only send in his waddling ganders to remove me) was that it strengthened his hubris. My notion was to force him to one side or the other, then see what he would do. This is what happened. When his sexual scandal did appear, I could point to the warning factors leading up to it. By continuing to ignore them, he achieves greater progress in moving backwards, with more refined manipulative skills, except on the unwilling. And that could very well be the only warning he acknowledged receiving, having told the still small voice to shut up once too often.

That the Evangelical Definition of Family, so Trumpeted, is a Deception, an Absolute Deception of the First Order

The sons of Constantine trod in the footsteps of their father, with more zeal and less discretion. The pretenses of rapine and oppression were insensibly multiplied; every indulgence was shown to the illegal behavior of the Christians; every doubt was explained to the disadvantage of Paganism (p. 423 MLE).

Picture a doctor who for ten years, according to his patients, has been a good doctor. He is so committed to his work he stays up late at night, then oversleeps and has to run to catch his train to an almost inaccessible region every morning. A growing yearning for a wife and family is taking hold, but he is unsure that he could at once properly take care of both a family and patients. No, he decides, a serious doctor must be pater familias. He marries. She assists him wonderfully in his practice so they both must catch the same train in the morning. Hand in hand they run to the train and only occasionally do they miss it. Yet the doctor is happier now, though he suffers at the thought of cellphoneless patients waiting long hours for his arrival. A ch is born and more trains are missed. Now some of his patients are gone, but he is heartened that his growing daughter can grab his hand as they run for their departure. However, they are slower than before, more time is missed, and as his despair grows at the thought of former days, he pushes it aside, fathers another child then settles into consulting from home those patients with the means to buy a ticket to see him.

This demonstrates approximately how evangelicalism corresponds to the Christianity of the New Testament.

What is essential to all Christian teaching is the imitation of Christ, and that means to move heaven and earth to remain single, to take the leap of faith to foreign lands if necessary to preserve this crucial element of Christlikeness. If in the most earnest effort one has tested oneself to the point of despair, when heaven itself will not budge, where one dares to thrust his fist in the face of God because one cannot escape the night voices calling for a life-long companion, then Abrahamic in excruciating obedience (waiting for the salvation of his Lord), he gives himself over (now joyfully) to marriage. He is not able to thank Him enough for the comfort of this divine concession.

Paul knew well the weakness of the flesh, and being pestered on all sides to yield on singleness, did, with the warning that marriage would constrain one's ministry. But he himself never took advantage of what evangelicals do to the point of nausea (evangelical dating services, online matchmaking and singles groups) and a lot of peripheral nonsense. Observing the fuss to marry and start a family, Paul would have appreciated the anecdote of the busy philosopher. When King Philip was on the verge of taking Corinth, the people of the city were in a frenzy of useless activity. Diogenes took immediate note and started wheeling his bathtub vigorously through the city. Questioned as to why he answered that he wanted to be like everybody else, and commenced to pushing the tub for he did not wish to be indolent amid so much busyness.

This is the relation of the enthusiastically churched-fed by the clergy-to marriage, what the New Testament views as a providential gift of last resort. Where the parable falls short is that Diogones knew well what he was doing, whereas the evangelical is merely falling into line.

Down the road three miles from where I stay in Colorado Springs is one of the most magnificent fortresses against love and Christ's imitation in all of evangelicaldom, beating its competition two miles down in Haggard's vision, and that is Dobson's grand formulation of familial self-love, Focus on the Family. This tourist attraction with a Hilton next door is his knavish response to the Kingdom of God. Is this massive artifice what it means to seek the Kingdom, what is so obviously self-seeking? Is this adopting the mind of Christ, what is so manifestly a corporate mindset? Is this the care of orphans, trumpeting procreation? Does this portray the New Testament household, what is just another large edifice?

Indeed they fly with all the haste of despair, the young and weak in faith who allow themselves to be manipulated into creating a family. Once there they are all too eager to lap up the teaching of the pastors to raise their children in safe and secure environments, being properly instructed in Bible stories, prayer, church etc. etc. They sigh with relief when Dobson says missionaries ought not to bring up their children in foreign and backward lands. The conservatives were the first to start applauding this retreat from poor neighborhoods, for they are self-lovingly concerned with the protection of the group. Now, their darkness is exposed. But let just one member of an evangelical family become sincere and earnest, then such a character transformation takes place that the entire family is placed under extreme tension. Its as if Samson is showing the Philistine pillars to be vulnerable. Christ has given that earnest individual a new family. This new family creates a clash between Him and the worldly church, and that clash is first visited upon the evangelical family who have entirely bought into the corrupt pastor/priest's form of Christianity. The new, regenerated family is made up of those who are earnest and those alone. When that earnestness sets in there is a deep realization that the old household idols have been smashed. Now there are immediate consequences and new mothers, fathers, sisters and brothers have emerged (in the way one might be pulled from quicksand to solid ground).

And when this painful extraction has been accomplished, when one has established the new families of faith we are commanded to found and still find it not enough, if one absolutely (in the sense of the Absolute) must marry, then on, with joy, to this blessed union. But let us not continue this optical illusion that marriage is the first and greatest post-conversion gift of God, as the pairing masters, the clerics, do whose mortgage payments depend upon maintaining the illusion.

C.S. Lewis' portrayal of the single woman, whose earthly life was devoted to loving orphans, being crowned a princess in heaven with the adulation of both children and angels, could rightfully apply to that couple, just-married, attempting to decide how many children they should have. Being shown in a dream the children they would raise in heaven if they were to refrain from having their own, they decide it would be better to adopt, rather than risk losing this eternal privilege and enjoyment.

So at bedtime they went to their knees and asked God for some self-control, and in turn for unwanted children to be placed at their doorstep. Over the years, sure enough, their prayers were answered. When others inquired as to why the couple never had had their own children, the couple understood: they experienced a new birth loving children not of their own flesh.

When Christ says the poor you will always have with you and anytime you want to you can help them, orphans are included. Christ commands it, that the more we obey the command the more the desire to obey the command will grow. Otherwise we get a situation like we have now, where there are 143 million fatherless globally. This fact in no way hinders the pastor/priests from encouraging the procreative activities of their large flocks. Instead of hanging Do Not Disturb signs on their doors, which would be a more honest way of saying no to Christ's command to care for orphans, they by rote cry out 'Miracle of birth!', and this allows them to keep up the illusion that they are doing God and the earth a favor. The truth is that yet another human being must endure eighty years then possibly be lost forever because the parents could not show a little Christian continency.

The Haustafel, or house-table, Luther's term for the list of specific admonitions Paul wrote for wives, husbands, children and so on, is as true now as it has always been-for families already in existence. In the Christianity of the pastor/priests the meaning is inverted: Produce children, a lot of them with or without means, and then apply the Haustafel. So these shepherds of procreation, like Dobson, spend countless hours expounding on the Haustafel under the correct assumption that their millions are more than a little interested in creating more children. Blessed teachers of Christianity, these mature men of faith, of whom it could be said they are the insider traders of religion, thieves for stealing people's money certainly; they hold secrets too, hidden knowledge (the New Testament), and that makes them liars as well.

Beware then the context of Paul's admonitions! The Dutch priest moves into a slum in Rio, finding a baby abandoned inside his tent door, applies the Pauline demand in raising the child who calls him his father. The single woman, earnest to demonstrate Christianity, relocates then promptly befriends a host of desperate children. This is what it means to apply Ephesians to the present age, and nothing like the preaching/ teaching of the self-contained and sheltered.

Evangelical parents will not adopt many children and refugees because they are either willfully entrapped or find too much enjoyment in the suburbs, with their pastor's Hi-Ho-the-merry-o endorsement. The token response of the church to international adoptions mirrors evangelical leader's own partial recognition of some of Christ's commands. But when the church is the church there is a sacrificial movement toward one another then the weak, and now the world is truly turned upside down by the numbers of orphans and refugees (the pastor/priests insist on calling it a refugee crisis when it is in fact a moral crisis of the West) who are cared for as the Haustafel intended.

But if being like Christ within the family is rightly linked to salvation by faith, if Christ's love compels to the love of Christ, then church leadership has concluded that Christianity is not for them. So what to do? Turn the gospel into a suburban comfort zone, yes, twist the truth into an abyss-bound lie . . . which is Focus on the Family, the deception being: calling themselves Christians while living as pagans.

Dr. Dobson Goes on a Bear Hunt: A Parable Based on a Real Event

What is the difference between faith and the proclamation of faith?

. . . In the first ages of society, when the fiercer animals often disputed with man the possession of an unsettled country, a successful war against those savages is one of the most innocent and beneficial labors of heroism. In the civilized state of the Roman empire, the wild beasts had long since retired from the face of man and the neighborhood of populous cities. To surprise them in their solitary haunts [to] be slain in pomp by the hand of an emperor was an enterprise equally ridiculous for the prince and oppressive for the people (p. 64 MLE) (italics mine).

When I think of all these populist pastors, it is easier to lump them together as one man, a Henry VIII type, leaning back on his leather chair, biding his time until his next appearance, signing off on this project or that, listening to flattery about his latest act, statement, international initiative, or last Sunday's sermon. Restless, he moves on to his next engagement, perhaps lingering a little to see if one has another question, but always endeavoring to be the principal reference. Fear of boredom is an excellent motivater, and plump rulers know best how many diversions there are to pass the hours.

Rest and recreation pose the same challenge. It is not only that the jolly pastor must find entertaining ways to work off that exhaustively fine buffet, but he also has to find something that inspires sermons, interviews, devotions, etc., for after all the evangelical public awaits, hat in hand, for that word of inspiration and assurance that will lead them home.

Which is why, of course, Dr. Dobson goes on bear hunts, then returns to a Focus on the Family meeting to tell faithful employees to 'get over it' if they have a problem with it. But I will clothe his bear hunt in possibility, that something else happened on the hunt of which the uninformed were kept in the dark.

One recent spring morning a grizzly bear awoke from hibernation feeling rather lonely. When he went to the waterfall to catch fish near the other bears, he wanted to hear from them why it was bears did what they did; why they wrestled over females, left claw marks on trees, stood on their hind legs when threatened, ate so much and were generally solitary creatures. He was sincere in his desire to learn if there was another and better way.

He went above the bank to where the younger and stronger bears had surrounded an elder to alert and protect him, a rare thing in that species. It was to this elder he was directed. 'You do well to desire to know these things,' said the wise old bear. 'Go to the human beings, to whom the secrets have been bestowed, and among them you will find a small clan known as the Christians, whom we call the Creation Caretakers, and they will tell of the god. They will make known what your ancestors have longed to know for a million sleeping times. I am too old to undertake this perilous trek with you, having wasted my youth in the cool waters catching fat fish, searching for the juiciest berries and forever looking for the most comfortable caves. But the bears who have gone, it is said, have returned to be the mightiest in wisdom and leadership, though some have not come back.

You were meant to serve in a noble capacity, therefore your instruction will take a long time. Wait three resting periods, then embark. In the meantime train well, and do not run toward those things that make you forget what you are searching for; the garbage cans, a zoo life that can give you amnesia, gorging beyond your need and engaging in the pleasures of fighting and mating. Beware the lusty, indolent ways, then you will be disciplined enough to run from the men in silly hats carrying long sticks, the stickmen. Bolt from them, for their desire is only to stand as gods over your dead body, thinking they know good and evil.

Walk slowly only toward those walking alone or with a book-the ones with cameras you can ignore-or perhaps a few will be sitting in a circle reading from the book. The books may be on their laps with their heads down. Do not let their singing and laughter frighten you, but let this encourage your approach.

Restrain yourself and do not for joy of discovery rush toward them. If they stand, do not stand with them, for this will frighten them. If they run, do not run after them, as they will only fall into fetal positions and pretend they are asleep, and there is no reasoning with them. Remain calm and make your gestures peaceful, lowering your head and gazing around lazily. The boldest of them will speak with you gently, until he comes to know you; then he will talk with you as he would with one of his own.'

Now the bear could understand everything the elder told him, and took to readying himself for his encounter with the humans. Two things he remembered well, like the Chinese emperor who told his counselor to remind him of a critical matter every hour; to be different and better than the other bears-which is training in bravery-and not to become impatient, for what he would learn would affect the bear clan for ten thousand resting periods to come. He had heard of his cousins the polar bears, who were being starved and driven to odd behaviors by the heat the stickmen had brought to the cold lands, now seeing the human only as enemy.

So he began, advancing into the battle against his own instincts. Avoiding conflict over females, he took one wife. He loved her as Christ loved the church; and remained with her, normally something bears never do. He even played gently with the cubs, after first being warned off by her, since she had seen what adult males do to cubs when they were jealous.

He did not know how hard his life would become. He could hear the other bears calling him a Contrary. He knew what that meant. They were referring to the choice of certain American Indians, many summers ago, to do everything backwards. The Indian would avoid paths in order to walk through bushes. Ask him a favor and he would do the opposite. He washed in dirt, dried off in the water and so on and so forth. The bears at the time would stare at the Indian stupified, until he would comically attack, sitting on his horse backwards, facing the tail end; finally the bears would flee, laughing, into the deep forest. So these stories were passed down and rose up again in the form of ridicule at his expense.

He endured their taunts and continued to fight off his drives. It meant less food, less wandering time, no time sharpening his claws, all of which sharpened his character, as one who rules himself is greater than one who rules an empire. His wife pleaded with him to indulge himself a bit more because she was concerned about his physical and mental health; she saw that he suffered so, but he said nothing. The harder he was on himself, the more (she quietly suspected) he loved the thought of learning the secrets. Wonderful! Yet one thing was clear: he was on his own. No other bear joined him, though some spoke openly about it and even bowed their heads as he walked by. His wife encouraged him in the ways she knew how; but help came to him in ways he had not expected-the elder said this would happen-it came from an unexplainable quarter. He no longer wept at what he had lost, but was holding up.

The third resting period neared; he retreated into his den with his wife, the cubs having long gone; he knew upon waking he must go.

He awoke. In some ways he felt a cub again, eager to listen and learn. He did recall regrettable impulsive behaviors which were human-like actions. He hated the notion of ever repeating them, such as wounding a bird and attacking the deer that defended her fawn. He sought to act upon a thoughtful youth, upon a loving playfulness, upon finding a role model, upon defending the bear with a limp; to make the effort at going back in time through recollection, then action. He grew ashen, reeling at the thought of doing just as the other bears like using size to oust a mother and her cubs from her den, feeling the same about this as any shy young girl would about betraying too early her love for the young man. These thoughts are what he held to as he began walking.

Though his wife barely understood, she mourned at seeing him go, for it is not a simple matter to let go of one whose love has improved and grown so, and hers for him. The other bears were not sorry, and in fact some had been calling for his departure more passionately, the elder having since died. To leave the bear clan seen as irrelevant to most, hated by some, then to have the few bears who knew him well enough to depend upon, abandon him (their present comfort and hope of greater comfort was of greater value than a friendship that promised none of this) meant they spoke of him no more. It was as if he had never been born. Not surprisingly, his former friends began to imitate the other bears.

He walked on, looking back not with longing as Lot's wife, but as one who looks back at his first school. 'Abandon the journey?' he asks. 'No, spirit compels me forward. By the god Himself! Come what may, as if the decision had been made for me, yet I make the decision; let the hunger, loneliness, dogs and stickmen come, I am constrained from Above, not as in the enthusiasm of first realizing my task, but in a decisive headstrong way, nothing can turn me away now' but there was a foreboding that accompanied his thoughts, as if descending into darker waters. It was as if his abandonment did not stop there, the losses would not cease, his unexplainable help withdrew . . .

He waited patiently, yet endlessly for some solace, for the berries, nuts and honey of his old home, for a deeper den too cold for the flies. What he got was hunger, biting mosquitos under his eyes, fallen trees as shelter that dripped dew and rain, vicious dogs that snapped at his heels; but it had not entered his mind, until now, that it should be the god Himself who hid His face from him-or so it seemed.

Perhaps success awaited him at the end of his journey, perhaps not. His thoughts swung from the people of the god being near, which quickened his step, to wondering if he would ever find the holders of secrets (meaning faith), then he would slow, feeling weary and these people too hard to find. Thus he held up, not knowing that in an agonizingly slow manner he was acquiring the secrets and becoming what he was told he would become.

The years passed. The bear, now old with graying snout, still ran yet with lungs and legs heavy with age that caused him to stumble. Wiser, he saw the stickmen before they saw him. He had suffered deeply with no hoped-for result, but with the years of holding out he had become a miracle among bears, a friend of the fighting badger, desiring little meat, gazing for an hour at the birds of the air and the lilies of the field, taking only what the bees had left behind, eating only the nuts the squirrels had dropped, careful never to disturb a nest and self-accusatory when nature flew from him. He never thought of himself as anything more than a meek unprofitable servant of the god, who only saw his own deficiency in relation to Him.

Faraway in a land to the south, the Right Reverend-de-facto-former-Chaplain-to-the-White-House Dr. James Dobson was skimming through his New Testament and his glance happened to fall upon these words of Christ: 'It is the Father's good pleasure to give you the kingdom.'

He began to ponder what the words meant. 'The Father has given us the kingdom! Well, the kingdom here cannot mean heaven, because we are not dead yet. The early church, though well-intentioned, misunderstood the hearty impact of Christ's words, which must be accepted quite literally. They must be interpreted for the here-and-now. And what is our primary example of the meaning of the Kingdom? Why Genesis of course, where man was given the command to rule over every living creature that moves on the ground.'

Now things are really set in motion (!), for this personally advantageous understanding had implications for creation across the board. A spine tingling thrill reverberated throughout the virile, male evangelical community in America, for now man could-thank you Lord-expand upon any previous definitions of Christian rest after work. Now, with a clear conscience before God, man, and animal, hunt Christianly.

Meanwhile in his office, Dr. Dobson made a few phone calls, aid was procured to purchase a few high powered rifles, and voila, this well-armed pair of saintly hunters were set to go. And what is the most dangerous game they will pursue, or have the misfortune of being pursued by? O how empty the world would be if we could not marvel at the courage of those who emulate our ancestors, who had only the spear by which to cut down the ferocious bear. This tiny remnant, a remnant for the truth, these representatives of the holy priesthood held a bit of an advantage though over their ancestors, and not only the scoped rifle. They had the sacred scripture itself, a sure guarantee of success in the world of bear hunting.

They embarked, led of course by the Reverend-good-natured Dr. Dobson, who managed to keep the general public, his employees and the press ignorant of his intention, so as to preserve their rest.

It must be said here, unless anyone should think these men to be weak men of faith, that upon finding a proper campsite they got down on their knees and prayed that Christ may grant them hunting prowess and good fellowship.

They believed the bear to be an altogether simple beast, easy to track and deceive. The nature programs show them rather unconcerned before photographers and filmakers. But even the subtlest human observation must mean no more to the bear than the flies around his nose. 'Please excuse my troubling you, but I'm trying to make a living,' says the fly. 'You are of no account to me,' was the reply. Only let the man's effort be directed toward gaining the bear's attention by doing something remarkable, such as the three wise men of whom Herod took notice because they undertook a dangerous journey based on a wonderful rumor. Perhaps the bear realizes a comfort and security when a good man is near (by chasing the stickmen away), and so pays the good man greater attention. But assume the bear had been surrounded by cameramen its whole life, learning to pay them no heed, then one thinks the bear to be an exceedingly stupid animal, when a man approaches with what looks to the bear like another filming device, but in fact is a weapon.

Thus it is with believing bear hunters, who are more than a little happy to show off their new bearskin rug, and for the evangelical throng to see that Christ grants everything earthly to those whom He loves. But is this to be the fate of our long-suffering, well-trained and disciplined old bear of the forest?

It was early in the morning, with the brightest star having assumed its place in a dark blue blanket, on a day that the Lord had made. Dobson and friend were on the lookout. Running through their minds were the Old Testament war stories, and they felt themselves amid one now as they crept through bear country. Dobson, ever the patriot, could not help but think of General George Armstrong Custer ambushing a Cheyenne village at the same hour. Instructions were given then they split up and moved forward; their jaws were set and the adrenalin flowed. Cellphones were switched on to signal silently, Bibles were placed in backpacks, the God of Elisha's bears was invoked and the hunt was commended to Providence. All was made ready for conflict with the world, except one thing - Biblical truth.

This was a trivial matter. What did concern them though was that the game should be played properly, so that every tiny detail lent credence to the delusion that they were actually engaged, like Christ, in real spiritual conflict with the world; in this regard they are like Muslims who throw rocks at a wall that represents the devil.

Now they walked a long time through the upper valleys parallel to the hills, but far from any viewpoints, and so they made a sharp turn to attain a high point and gaze in all directions with binoculars.

They were not needed. When they found the height, one could note on their faces the immensity of the panorama laid out before them. Their expressions were of polite reserve mixed with awe. It was the normal look of men who had spent most of their lives in tony offices and were now far north on an excursion, believing the Alaskan wild to be there for them to master, rather than the vital home it was for a vast constellation of animals.

But that sight made them step back and steady themselves against a tree. Dobson's head began to jerk some, unwilling to accept what his eyes were telling him. Before them stretched an endless sea of undulating misty green, a hundred miles in all directions, with rare wisps of smoke writhing into the air breaking up the monotony. While living on the edge of the Sahara I have seen the unrelenting sand; that, the oceans and the stars are the only things comparable.

They had already walked five miles, but here was the odd part: other than birds rustling in the trees, they still had not seen one creature on any side. Could it be they were searching backwards?

The reader may anticipate what Dobson did next. He laid down his gun, sat down, removed his hat, took out his Bible and began to thank the Master for the humility brought on by the magnificence of His creation. He went on to thank Him for the trial they were being put through and for the hope of bear that led them there. They implored Him for success, frustrated and fatigued as they were, with bitter sighs, enough to make angels and little children bow their heads.

They were still sitting when they saw their first bear dart into a thicket at two hundred yards; the old bear had seen them first with books in hand and heads down, exactly what the elder had told him to look for. He wanted to tease them into coming to him, remembering not to rush for joy at seeing the answer to his prayers. The men rose up, careful not to make any sudden movements, and hid themselves behind the larger trees. Though he could smell them, he did not see Dobson creeping closer to the bush with his Bible in one hand (in his anxiety he had forgotten to put it down) and his rifle in the other.

Having learned the language of the humans from bears who had traveled south, his moment had finally arrived. But not quite. Experience had made him wary and he did not reveal himself yet, though he longed to.

Dobson knew it would be suicide to head into the thicket, so he thought to cajole the bear out into the open. 'Come to me, brother bear, for you are better than us men; by not attacking us while we sat, you have repaid us with good, whereas men have repaid you with evil. And you have shown us today that you have dealt well with us, in that you did not destroy us when the Lord put us into your claws. For if a bear finds its enemy, will he let him go away safe? So may Christ award you today for what you have done. We know that you are king of Alaska, and that your God and mine has established it in your claw. Swear to us then by the Lord that you will not attack us by day or night, and that you will not cut off our ministry from the land.' And the bear, moved by his words and absorbed by thoughts of this Christ, swore to him.

Now the bear, humming a song to the god, as he did every day, emerged. Dobson and friend had their sharpshooters ready; they opened fire from both sides thinking they could not have a wounded bear on their hands. And the now mortally wounded bear found it within himself to crawl back into the bush.

The men approached the bush cautiously, as they could not know the bear to be entirely dead-and everyone knows it takes a long time for a strong bear to die-though there was much blood on the ground. While they were discussing what to do next, a panting, baritone voice arose out of the thicket, 'How are you a Christian? How do you find your hope in God?' Dobson thought this an odd deathbed question, since all Christendom knew him as a writer and speaker of no mean reputation, and that of all people he had the right to answer in the affirmative. Thus, 'Yes, I am a Christian.' 'Tell me how?' replied the bear, 'for there is no evidence of it, and here I lie,' gasped the bear. 'Faith saves lives, shows itself restless for life. How can you say that you and your friend here have the real wounding restlessness of faith? How have you shown yourself different than other men in the land? How has your renunciation been visible?' this was said in spurts through a coughing fit. Dobson's response: 'I am justified by faith alone.' 'Justified, justified,' mocked the bear, you speak thus to me after this.' By now some of the smaller animals who smelled death had drawn near to the bear. 'You watch over each other' whispered the bear to the badger and the squirrel. Turning his large head the other direction, he continued to Dobson, 'If you had had faith, you would not have come here with guns, for somewhere in your book it must say I will show you my faith by my works. Does this mean nothing to you, that if one has faith it is visible and clear immediately? Justification is a fine word opening fire.

'Trust me, millions will tell you I have faith.'

'Shut up, and let me die in silence.'

'But what about all my books, of which my latest is a bestseller? There is your evidence.'

'Being shot is not enough, but must I also tolerate a fool in my final moments? Well, good for you that you are a skilled poet on faith and family, but it only demonstrates that you are a poet; despite your denials, that is all you are, and no man of faith. It means you have done eternal harm, a yawning chasm from any good you think you have done. A legendary bear, before being speared in Rome's coliseum, heard Nero recite poetry, and said it was not bad . . .' And with this he became what he willed to become.

With prolonged anguish such as no other bear had chosen to live, with efforts which could only lead to one possible conclusion, his desire was transformed. In sufferings not even the starved polar bear could approach, was he moved by the god to carry on a life the absolute opposite of his element. And to have him searching for truth in Christendom with too few Christians means being shot, certainly, but more than that it meant denying and dying to what gave the grizzly his name, so that he could leave behind animals of whom he said 'Now I call you my friends.'

As for Dr. Dobson, the fact that it was the Father's good pleasure to give him the kingdom notwithstanding, tears began to well up in his eyes, and yes they came from the heart . . . as they do in Hollywood.

Beware of Them That are Utterly Predictable

It must be ingeniously confessed that the ministers of the Catholic [or Christian] church imitated the profane model which they were impatient to destroy. The most respectable bishops had persuaded themselves that the ignorant rustics would more cheerfully renounce the superstitions of Paganism if they found some resemblance, some compensation in the bosom of Christianity. The religion of Constantine achieved, in less than a century, the final conquest of the Roman empire: but the victors themselves were insensibly subdued by the arts of their vanquished rivals (p. 538-39 MLE) (italics mine).

What I have written is quite simple to understand. Evangelical leaders overlook, in practice deny, shun, blunt anything to do with the imitation of Christ. This is clear to anyone who takes the time to read the New Testament and compare it with what is in front of their own eyes. To those with some knowledge of the medieval church one may say these leaders are as much connected to the New Testament as medieval popes were to St. Francis, or in this age as much as the speechmaking toastmasters are to a real Christian transformation. What passes as Christianity now does not approach the fantastic collision that marked the life of the early Christians against the empire. But Dobson's life (his flattery of Trump was a reflection of his love for conservatism) could not possibly be understood as a collision with the age. If one were to argue Dobson's life does collide with the age, then one must also say that a real Christian leader is a big builder and a shrewd marketer, and that this means a collision with the age. This, from a New Testament standpoint, is as realistic as a deluded man, believing himself rich, handing out counterfeit money.

How despicable is the influence of this society of hypocrites, the well-salaried pastor/priests of America, what convulsions arise. Or must. But why do they not arise? Because whenever there is an outcry against them then massive numbers are sent in to claim that nothing is wrong. The pastors actually doing something, in rural areas, trailer parks, reservations, core cities, or faraway lands are so consumed with the needs at hand they have no time to protest the sheer apathy of the American church. Those who do are set aside as radicals, social gospelers, communists, socialists, or an unChristian exaggeration.

This is why I will not let church leaders ignore me, knowing full well their ardent followers, with all the distinction of a flock of geese, will believe I am just another ranter. Being squawked at to death by geese is one way to die, but being ignored while sitting in the middle of the street is quite another. I prefer the geese, so I will not go away.

Any serious observer can expect the pastors to fight back with . . . a loud silence. When I say, for example, that the teaching of Christianity for our age does NOT point to abortion as the primary evil, but to malnutrition and hunger, nuclear war and climate change (caused by a lawless Christendom) then you would think the pastoral swashbucklers would marshal the force of numbers to defend themselves. This they will not do. This cowardly clique of well-spoken thieves will hide like naughty children under the covers of abortion, religious freedom, and gay marriage. Why? Because they know, O reader, they know all too well that their lives are not at stake by attacking abortion/gay marriage and defending religious freedom. How effeminate of the pastor/priests to take on homosexuals and women, whose reputation is to fight to their last drop of blood using . . . uncivil language.

About the most one could expect from the comfortable pastors is an attack on my credibility as a Christian, in other words they will respond as they always have throughout the course of their compromised history, like scorned women. A thug, when exposed, will at least respond murderously. Not so the church leaders, who have been exposed for their cringing fear of losing what has become so dear to their hearts, that warm glow that comes from the approval of the crowds and the handshake with a political leader. It is fear of men, fear of men, fear of men, that leads them to cower behind their robes and whimper instead of admitting honestly, like men, that the New Testament and the early church are just too hard for them to live up to. So if they were honest, it could mean backing down, changing, and that would be a very dangerous matter for those whose main aim in life is a glittering career.

Now, if I do not alter my criticism, perhaps some pastors

will fire back. How? Let the reader beware, for my sentence will seem unduly harsh; so very brutal that parents will want to cover their children's ears. If I do not stop the attack, then-here it comes-I am to be invited to attend their church. Terrors! Yes, if I do not change my ways, I would be welcomed into the anonymity of the 11:00 service, then forced to listen to the theater representation of the pastor as he is moved to tears by his description of OTHERS suffering for the Truth, and how he himself would suffer IF-note this life and death conditional-yes, IF it is asked of him. And I, the transgressor, being unaware of all the wonderful things their church is doing should be there to see it for myself. Either that or just spiritually waste away (apart from the meat of the Word provided by the pastor), not being able to contribute my small offering which would put a chicken in the pot for the pastor and his loved ones. Further, let my punishment be extended so that every Sunday I would be welcomed to a new church and given a tour of the building(s). The Inquisition itself could not come up with such a refined torture. Yet all of this I brought on myself, for when every Tom, Dick, and Harry was preaching the unity of Christendom I was preaching division, and that is what I will be branded as. What happens after that is in Christ's hands.

With respect to an honest counterattack by the conformed church, it is another matter altogether. What shape the attack would take is beyond me. The current situation is so spiritless that it is hard to imagine a church choir or bellringers becoming passionate about anything other than voting, not to mention effeminate men in long robes, the pastors, getting riled up.

They may appear to be passionate behind the pulpit, but they have a real economic interest in not taking legal action. This is what I have already encountered, for when I speak outside their expensive buildings, either security is called to remove me (which is unnecessary for the crowds avoid me anyway) or the pastor thanks me for my opinion and skulks away.

The American church is so flabby and spiritless that its leadership knows it has been caught in a lie, therefore it will do all within its power to keep the matter out of the public eye and away from the courts. It is a risk to confront the monstrosity who are the reigning American church authorities; though the adversary were a gadfly, it may be enough to disturb the whole herd's march. Where I have spoken out people continue to attend the churches as if nothing had happened. It is only because a man like Dobson has the worldly resources to protect his people from hearing often and clearly that their worship in this way is blasphemy. Dobson's manner in dealing with me forms a perfect window into the use of worldly shrewdness to duck-and-cover oneself and others from New Testament demands. During the 2004 election I wrote him a letter telling him he needed Christian character transformation etc. I received back exactly what I expected, a form letter requesting money. The next move was to confront him personally, but the jetsetter was in Washington (a place he loves and it loves him), so I admonished his assistant to sell their buildings then begin house churches among the poor and to relay that message to his boss.

He thanked me for sharing my thoughts-this constant smiling rejection-and assured me he would do so. I was bent on making the Right Reverend doctor responsible before God so I returned to his megaplex, with reluctance yet necessity, to speak out at the exit at quitting time. I knew that security would arrive shortly; I had to be brief and to the point. I was and they did, and thus ended my fabulously unsuccessful ministry at Focus on the Family. But I was not through yet, seeing that he had probably heard nothing of what I had to say. I then sent a letter to one of the more independently minded local weeklies attacking his claim that he and Focus were acting Christianly. Again no response from Focus or Dobson. One wonders if a situation could possibly become more demoralized, for a congregation has a right to think that a charge of heresy against its leader should be met with something other than a Philistine brush-off, evasion and quietism.

Anyone who sets out to confront the conformed church powerbrokers can expect the same treatment, every effort being made to keep the proclaimer away from the young and those who may listen, flicking him off as if he were a fly on the shoulder. That, or by characterizing him as a radical, altering his words, singling him out as one who considers himself above the church, accusing him of pride. This has been my experience and in every case I have rejected legal remedies.

It is not just that my easy-going personality refuses to actively defend itself (I have an inherent dislike for conflict), but that I have attempted to take an ethical/religious view of matters and not wasted a moment preparing any legal action. This I will continue to do, for what does one who applies to the courts have in mind? Finite concerns, for one's career and economic prospects are now at stake. This is what one is expected to do if one has means, and this is why laziness and water-cooler gossip also show tremendous growth potential. People simply trust the courts to weed out the truth while they sit and speculate, instead of finding out for themselves the credibility of the accused and the accuser and what each side is fighting for.

I have absolutely no intention of letting people off the hook in this way because it is their God-given obligation to find out. In my early thirties a fine chance to litigate arose when I was released from a counseling position at a hospital for advising a teen not to have an abortion. If I had chosen to get mixed up with any number of evangelical organizations (who would have legally taken up my case) I may have won the right to return to work. The notion of applying worldly and temporal means never occurred to me, only that this youth had been made ethically/religiously responsible and more importantly her infuriated doctor (I hesitate to use the term).

Afterwards none of my colleagues ever bothered to discover the truth of my sudden departure. This goes to show that people much prefer gossiping over coffee to any serious effort. My approach to exposing the nincompoopism and misleadership of evangelicaldom has been through a direct personal confrontation by spoken word if possible and written when not. There was a time when this sort of confrontation evoked a reaction, blood would have boiled and harsh words exchanged, if not more. In our age what happens to the detective who reveals the hideous nature of the crime? His evidence is immediately declared irrelevant and ignored. This is precisely what occurred when, in front of a small crowd at a bookstore, I calmly told Jenkins and the late Tim Lahaye (they of the enormously popular Left Behind book series) that their massive output of literary conjecture was, Christianly, well-written heresy. Yes, I had just verbally slapped their faces and now beware O reader again for the cataclysmic response-they expressed appreciation for my opinion and moved on. This is what you get from two men who commit their whole existence to guesswork, (dancing around Biblical warnings not to obsess on the end of days) engaging in a delicate two step that moves lightly around collisions. Who, my reader, in all of religious history has answered the charge of heresy with a compliment? No, these two did not go to the marketplace to address like Paul true and false religion, but to cash in on their sparkling imaginations, and judging by the crowd they did very well.

The fact that the pastor walks away from me, church folk go the long way around and security arrives quickly is something I take as progress by New Testament standards. Clearly I am not altogether eager to rid myself of this treatment should I desire further progress. When I bring the grievance that the New Testament has against the American church before the eyes of its main offenders, I am not stunned to have them pretend there is no offence taken. But to have those most damaged by the pastor's conformity, the congregations, defend him so, then I am bound to feel a sting. Yet I am told not to be overcome with worry, not to wear my emotions on my sleeve, only to move ahead with the confrontation. That for every time I am treated this way there is a certain infinite profit from it.

This is the intelligence I am privy to from my hard working detective. He speculates that you, my reader, have taken it to heart that the American definition of the evangelic is a scam, and have gone on to argue it with your pastor. The consequences for the both of you would look something like this: The pastor returns to his suburban home. He kisses his wife, plays with his children then watches the evening news. When dinner is over and the children are excused, he tells his wife 'One of the church members came in today and kept insisting we sell the church, and homes too, and be a house church in a deprived neighborhood. He referred to the New Testament and the historical record repeatedly. I must say the man made sense.'

For just a moment he sees a flash of disbelief in his wife's face. 'Mark dear, what could you be thinking? We are settled here, it's a quiet neighborhood and the house payments are reasonable. And the children-their education, their safety-then there is the church, we simply cannot abandon them. The suburbs need churches too. What would happen if all the churches left the suburbs?'

Mark finishes his coffee, goes to his study and examines some commentaries for his Sunday message. Over the ensuing year his church takes in another hundred members from a nearby development and the building committee is considering expansion-and Mark had just been directly confronted with the demands of Christianity upon his life!

Be warned then, congregant reader, of the willful stupidity you are up against! And America is a dime a dozen with these nincompoops.

The pastor, a teacher of the gospel, craving comfort gives in to the most obvious of seductions. Why consider any change when a decent salary is assured? Why upset your loving wife, the epitome of a pastor's wife, who helped build your family and so propelled your career? Let us leave it at that for him.

But let me return to you, faithful congregant, who dared to take His demands seriously, after living a long time with a bad conscience. The pastor now avoids you and in private counsels others to do the same. This leads you to re-examine yourself, if perhaps it is you who are in error, and you tremble. You press on in humility and sincerity, demanding of yourself greater sacrifice and gentleness, which prompts even greater suspicion among the leadership. You are accused of being divisive, the snake in the grass, because your actions and words indicate that Christianity is a way of life. That it does not just reside in the heart ('My Heart Christ's Home') where perhaps there it remains under house arrest. But in fear and trembling you practice what you already know, and that is to be a Christian means to suffer for the truth. You face choices now of ultimate concern, yet this is not what your mind rests on. It is on the Exemplar, without whom you could not have made it this far. Indeed, the God-man has forewarned you that love is not loved, but hated. You carry this image with you into your abandonment and new life.

This sadness does not mean isolation and embitterment. You have come too far with Him for that. This is why you preface your defense before the congregation not with 'I think that . . .' but with 'The New Testament's view is . . .' then comes the suspicion and accusations. You may quote Luther and

Bonhoeffer to the Protestants and St. Francis and Vatican II to the Catholics, hesitating only to accuse yourself. Further, others accuse you of exaggeration, of not searching for middle ground, of denying what has become over the centuries a secular religion, the American church's exceptionalism. With the image that love is not loved before your eyes you press on, bidden by Christianity which promises no desolation, but that a new family will be given to you.

Such is the tension between yourself and the conformed pastor/priests. Believing that you are not acting in vain you venture out. You will be provided either with direct and personal training in Christianity (the more common New Testament means) by those more mature in faith, or privatissime. If you put forward the effort and are diligent then you will be able to hold out against all neglect, gossip and accusations, even those you level against yourself.

If you read this work and consider me a ranter, then you have not read it carefully enough; if you have read it and believe I am on the right road then I am under compulsion to warn you of the import of taking my words seriously, if you decide not to let the attacks on your Christian character lead you slowly away. To become just like the others, in this you will find no shortage of encouragement.

A Sermon from the Bible, or, What Happened to the 3,000?

Do large numbers demonstrate that Christianity has come to America?

Before the structure of the church had risen two cubits above the ground, forty-five thousand two hundred pounds were already consumed; and the whole expence amounted to three hundred and twenty thousand: each reader, according to the measure of his belief, may estimate their value either in gold or silver; but the sum of one million sterling is the result of the lowest computation . Yet how dull is the artifice, how insignificant is the labor, if it be compared with the formation of the vilest insect that crawls upon the surface of the temple! (Penguin p. 487)

A young man, fresh out of seminary, having had to pay his own way by teaching in a ghetto, returns to his home church in his college town. He knew the building had been replaced by one much grander to accommodate the crowds. The senior pastor singles him out to preach, for he recalled the young man's efforts on behalf of the youth in an earlier day.

The day arrives. His friends, family, the pastoral staff, the core membership and new faces make up a sizable crowd of 3,000 in a cavernous sanctuary. The congregation is led through Bible readings, song, prayer and praise, before the young man is introduced. The sermon text for the day is read and flashed up on the screen, about children obeying their parents and fathers bringing them up in the training and instruction of the Lord.

Standing behind the pulpit, the young man stares at the passage, looks up and says:

This passage is a command and not a recommendation. I tell you now that we have been measured and found wanting (the crowd detects deep gravity in his voice and some begin to stir), for in the name of raising up our children in the Lord we worship a lie, a sheer lie (there is a murmur in the crowd, and the elder pastor begins to blanch). All this is not Christianity (pointing his finger in a circular direction around the building), whatever name you call it, it is not Christianity.

Look at this magnificent building. Beautified lies (some of those sitting in the front rows get up). People learn only beautified lies by being brought here to worship, Christianity not being a beautified building, but a way of life (the pastor's face reddens, someone shouts out). Young people, believe me when I say that Christianity is suffering for the faith (more shouts follow, some parents are seen getting up with their children).

He sustains the assault: (his voice projecting out over the growing commotion). Many of you are pleased with your small group Bible studies. I tell you this is tokenism and not enough. If you would be serious, sell your large homes, move to dirt poor neighborhoods, and THERE have your Bible studies, giving the greater portion of your money away as you go. It is THERE you must be church together in simplicity, sharing and proximity (the pastor starts up, half the congregation stands at once, a group of young people sit transfixed).

The young man grips the pulpit:

Teach your children truthfully and well. Take in the single mother with child. Bring in orphans, widows and refugees. Invite the stranger into your home. Expose the darkness of concentrated wealth/militarism (younger and stronger deacons arrive to assist the pastor, along with a security guard carrying a gun) and the violence against creation, which launches a direct attack on your Creator.

The young man stands his ground: Now you know what you are to do (shoved aside with force, his voice carries long and far) and may God guide you in examining your true intentions toward your family (he is finally hustled off the platform).

Now, who is left from the 3,000? The youth group in the front, who cannot take their eyes from the young man. Another small group of adults with special needs sits, awaiting a sign from their teacher to move, but the teacher, who has been nodding her head and saying 'yes', stays. A sullen youth with hair covering his eyes and pants slung low, leans forward in his chair. An elderly man and more elderly women dot the sanctuary, perhaps seven. An equal number of apparently single men and women remain, lost in thought. Three couples, one wife pregnant, prepare to depart, and all are silent. An African American woman is slowly readying her child to leave, her mind elsewhere. A black couple in African dress are leafing through their Bible. No one is left on the platform. Of the original crowd, some 50 abide.

Yes, this is what you call a revival.

A Faith Not Repented of

A decent portion [of money] was reserved for the maintenance of the [clergy]; a sufficient sum was allotted for the expenses of the public worship, of which the feasts of love, the agapae constituted a very pleasing part. The whole remainder was the sacred patrimony of the poor [and] to alleviate the misfortunes of prisoners and captives, more especially when their sufferings had been occasioned by their firm attachment to the cause of religion . . . smaller [and poorer] congregations were cheerfully assisted by the alms of their more opulent brethren . . . The Pagans acknowledged the benevolence, of the new sect (p. 266 MLE) (italics mine).

Luther wrote somewhere that faith is a restless thing. No believer would deny this obvious truth. Yet we must ask what exactly is meant by the term 'restless thing.'

To be restless in faith is to engage in works that matter. To sell that expensive home (expensive relative to third world economies) and give the widow's mite, as much as your faith allows-to the point where it stings-to those in need. This restless thing of giving ought not be accomplished through the international banking system, but face to face or through the hand of a trusted friend. Another restless thing: the more mature believer confronts the conformed evangelical authority with the New Testament demand, though the pastor/priest will probably walk away or call security. American church leadership is so fit/flabby most will not care what you say or do, in which case a restless move would be to go where Christianity is directly despised (e.g. jihadist strongholds), and be done with these false guides and their smiling rebuffs.

To engage in a restless thing is to point out to church laity the early church's implementation of the forbidden callings (what Paul would call the unclean things) such as taking up arms or making them, politics, court judgeships, environmentally destructive jobs (think oil drilling, logging, uranium mining etc.), vocations as bureaucrats-all forbidden by the New Testament's definition of what it means to be a Christian.

Compassion is demanded, to the extent the worldly churchmen will believe you are almost intoxicated. For then Christendom's token philanthropy (e.g. Compassion International with their palatial headquarters) of fundraisers, tithes,and offerings are exposed for what they are, play Christianity and a parody of giving. Thus we copy, in restless things, those lives the philosopher Pliny was referring to in his letter to the Emperor Hadrian. In it he notes the church hates warfare and financial ambition just as it takes in the orphan and cares for the elderly.

We are to bring refugees and the homeless into our own homes, as the church fathers spoke of an extra room for just this purpose. The young in faith will receive their training in the neighborhood of the serious church, to perhaps go to the ends of the earth to imitate what they learned at home. In this way the world is quietly moved by restless things.

Abandon all hope of a mass movement, that the newspapers will affirm it, or the public will acclaim you. Even less that these uberpopular pastors will endorse your efforts, for they have received their reward. Bonhoeffer's attack on cheap grace, on becoming a Christian without having to give up anything, has been compartmentalized into a few categories, all of which involve not having to give up anything of substance. Indeed, take this matter of the imitation of Christ seriously and you will see, the pastors will brand you a terrorist, as Haggard did referring to an anti-war act by a few courageous nuns.

Faith unto works, this is the New Testament. You must Christianly work as arduously as you can, humbly confessing your need for grace. This grace goes infinitely further than the grace of John Newton, the author of Amazing Grace who refused, post-conversion, to relinquish his investments in the slave trade. It goes infinitely further than that for these Hollywood pastor/priests, whose perdition is nearly assured. They will sing Amazing Grace as solemnly as children say the Pledge of Allegiance, and with about the same critical reflection. 'Peace, peace [they preach], when there is no peace,' has been the warning refrain that has echoed through the centuries, to those who will hear. This 'radical gift' of grace does not look at all radical when evangelical barkers lead works which are a religious expression of corporate America. It just looks mediocre.

The works of love, the tasks, the restlessness of faith-if these do not exist in a corporate/militaryAmerica, then faith has come to a standstill. Just as a ship that furls its sails lies dead in the water, so the pastor/priest who fails to act upon what is demanded of his leadership. Also the one who steers a safe course away from danger, never budging from port for the excitement of the trip. This is a fox-like cunning that avoids suffering, imitation, of the danger inherent in Christianity and the show ministers who know it. This is why they are so deeply imbedded in perdition unless they repent themselves.

The works of the priestly and pastoral class consist essentially of oratory, counseling, sermon or homily preparation, dispensing communion, hospital visits, doctrinal explication, 'hatching, matching, and dispatching,' along with the usual parlor talk and sofa rest. Life consists mainly in the abundance of things for mainstream evangelical authority. Haggard and his successor Brady's one hundred and thirty thousand dollar salary is not the exception in the larger churches, as remuneration is measured by corporate standards, i.e., numbers.

But Christians are characterized by act and being. For them proving they are Christians is what matters, and they are willing to go to the ugliest, most wretched places on earth to obtain it. The dross of the planet (they are not unaware of this), their quiet suffering cannot be completely hidden. This is apparent to anyone with the slightest depth. The spiritless West, when it cares to recognize these serious Christians, praises their boundless courage, not grasping what Christianity means FOR THEMSELVES. But other religions do, and call it a scandal and an offence.

The gospel says to not only be hearers of the word but doers of it. To admit that they (the pastor/priests) do not obey it, or to confess that they have done the exact opposite, this is too much for the suit-and-tie-and-robes nincompoops, these protoypes of hypocrisy. How wonderful (so they claim) it is to be under the love of God, to have the assurance of salvation. No matter to them Jesus' thirty three years were a torment no human could possibly understand, yet which He repeatedly testifies to. The works that brought on these agonized sighs of Christ are to be imitated, to the extent we are enabled. If not, then no excuses, only let us go to our knees with the humble admission we are not doing what we have been commanded to.

Now even carelessly indifferent unbelievers know from a cursory understanding of Christianitythat He would and did not kill, forbidding His followers to even hate. For three hundred years the church obeyed this teaching on punishment of disfellowship. What do the pastor/priests do now? They are in a real bind; this kind of preaching will not bring in the masses. Nor will it project their golden voices over the radio, send their delicate profiles into cyberspace or the air-waves, will not bring in donations, attract the attention of the press, secure the vote-to say nothing of what it will do to their career. No, this sort of preaching will not do at all. Well, how can a church leader make a living? In the name of Christ he blesses the sword. Yes, for Jesus sake boys, young men, girls and young women go to meet their God believing, with all the enthusiastic trust of youth, that their shepherds told them the truth.

Another example. In the book of James we are commanded to look after orphans, that this is true religion. No doubt James had seen Jesus storytelling, knowing that He would never have any children of his own. Again we see our pastor/priest trapped, for if he points out rightly that it is the parents' self-love that seeks to create after themselves, bearing children in an attempt to create eternal memories of themselves (at the expense of the orphan), then the congregation's numbers drop considerably. Clearly the command to be fruitful and multiply has been fulfilled. Also, this notion of the gift of life comes to us from the Old Testament (a less perfect covenant). But the pastor/priest's prestige is at stake, thus lies and hypocrisy triumph once again.

My evangelical reader, one whose roots I share and whose reality was my own, whose literature and teachers were mine and now yours, let us walk for a time and journey together through lands we once traveled. Let us walk by corpses we laid waste on the road, through smoking towns, collapsed houses and pockmarked streets. Back, back, we travel on the road of remorse, encompassed by old men sitting on ruins, lost in quiet despair, and old women wringing their hands by remains of homes where not a single stone remains in its place. Where children were, who pleaded for some boon that was never forthcoming. O reader, if you have embraced this evangelical leader, suburban evangelicalism or the middle class church then let us go back, yes, go back and through the gospel of suffering you will eternally gain Him, not knowing at the end of one's days the despair of a wasted life, truly being alone, of regret of what had been left undone, the uncertainty of salvation, nor the perpetual lament of Luther's melancholy refrain, 'O my sin, my sin, my sin.'

But the primitive Christian demonstrated his faith by his virtues; the writers of a later period celebrate the sanctity of their ancestors [and] display, in the most lively colors, the reformation of manners which was introduced into the world by the preaching of the gospel (p. 255 MLE) (italics mine).

The Present Age and Simeon Stylites: An Inexact Biography

What is Christianity without the works of love?

At the age of thirteen, the young Syrian deserted the profession of a shepherd and threw himself into an austere monastery. After a long and painful novitiate in which Simeon was repeatedly saved from pious suicide, he established his residence on a mountain about thirty or forty miles to the east of Antioch . . . he ascended a column which was successively raised from the height of nine to that of sixty feet from the ground. In this last and lofty station, the Syrian Anchoret resisted the heat of thirty summers, and the cold of as many winters . . . He sometimes prayed in an erect attitude, with his outstretched arms in the figure of a cross, but his most familiar practice was that of bending his meager skeleton from the forehead to the feet; and a curious spectator, after numbering twelve hundred and fourty-four repititions, at length desisted from the endless account. The progress of an ulcer in his thigh might shorten but it could not disturb this celestial life; and the patient hermit expired without descending from his column . . . The Christian world fell prostrate before [his] shrine(s) (p. 650 MLE) (italics mine).

It has been many years since Simeon Stylites invited me to be his biographer. I had been to his column so regularly the previous year I had acquired his confidence. He groaned that he was so full of enthusiasm for God that he could not bend and talk at the same time. He pleaded with me to bequeath to Christendom a summary of his high column reflections. I thought to humor him, that he may gain insight to himself, thus I consented.

At an early age he was taken from his sheep to a camp for young men where the monks spoke harshly and threatened him with every infernal agony unless he mended his ways. Then the tone changed, and the following day he was given several artfully decorated, hand copied scrolls of the New Testament and told this was the ultimate rule of faith by which the monks lived. What was he to do? Should he then live as the monks? Was he to be lost for eternity?

I asked him if, upon receiving the scrolls, he had consulted with an elder about this NT gift. He said yes, there had been another shepherd who had warned him against the monks abuse of it, of what needed to be done, of infinite responsibility-yes, the monks-against their Christianity.

He remained troubled. Then a vision occurred. He dreamt he sat with a host of eminent priests, monks, bishops, and clerics in a special tribunal. There he was made to choose his religious future. 'You may,' said Jerome, 'pastor a cathedral congregation in the splendid city of Antioch or wed a beautiful and godly wife who bears you many good children or shepherd a chapel in the lush groves of The Golan or become a monk in the desert. Choose the one you wish.' Neither hesitating nor blushing Simeon answered his dream companions thus: 'Holy and esteemed elders, it is my will that I should have the deep respect and adulation of the Christian masses and the prince, that they might reverence my bones.' Immediately the tribunal burst into applause. At that he knew his desires to be fulfilled, and acknowledged his contemporaries to be shrewd judges of worldly matters; since it hardly would have been appropriate to congratulate him for what everybody understands in secret.

He smiled to himself: What the masses sought was what had first caught his eye in the writing, the dainty artwork of the scrolls. If it was the extraordinary they wanted, and at the same time the evangelic, then that is what he would give them.

He admitted to a pang of conscience however, connected with the older shepherd who had warned him against the monks. The shepherd was not inactive, visiting the leper colony, hiring orphans to tend the flocks, giving wool and mutton to widows etc. Yet there was nothing sensational or novel in this, so the masses thought, it had been done before . . . Simeon recalled a priest, who preached only in front of the crowds, and then only when there were official dignitaries present. The less he appeared, the more refined his sermons, the more elegant the robes, the more esteemed the luminaries, the more of a crowd favorite he became. The lesson burned deep into his memory: that what the crowd desired was the sensual, a theater display. I will do something extraordinary, he thought, and I will begin at the monastery. On the eve of his departure he received a visitor, the old shepherd who addressed him directly: My son, perhaps you have not taken notice, but the believing shepherds have taken notice of you. Come to us, and attend our fellowship under the eucalyptus tree on our father's land, where you will be taught in the true Christian mysteries and trained in the way of Christ's shepherds. But first you must renounce in your life and heart the desire to become extraordinary in this life.

Then Simeon, humanly, became as one torn in two, as waves split equally, almost humiliated, seeing the invitation to return as an insult to his dream, something very bizarre. How dare they denounce his dream, that the shepherds may hold him up as an unChristian example. It appeared to him that they could do this, make him out to be an impudent clown for wanting to be something greater than the rest, perhaps withold communion from him and consign him to a life of anonymity. A commissioning by the shepherds to his monastic life he could understand; it would be grasped by the believing masses as a kindly gesture, a respectful nod to the authority of the monks. But as for leaving them just to be patronized, how absurd. What would people think of a young man who just tended sheep, lived quietly in a modest cottage and prayed with shepherds?

Thus he entered the monastery and there he came to despair, in despair over his ambition, because it had not died in him, for the possibility for greatness never presented itself. Then the monastery, the acute loneliness, the enforced silence, the drudgery of the labor and the prayers, the stone walls whose unchangeableness were as boring as his own life. The ambition, if he had achieved it, would have been to him his greatest joy, yet now he was lost without it; the well known man he could have been was now to him a worthless fellow, for his ambition was dying. That, or it had become a disgusting thing, since it had lied to him about its fulfillment. This death to the extraordinary, his ambition, he soon took on as his cross, a cross he was unable to bear. So he made a number of attempts at suicide, which he said-to please the monks-were for the sake of the gospel of suffering. But he failed in this too, for though he longed to get rid of himself, to consume himself, he found himself unable to complete the act, since a spark of the hope for the extraordinary remained in him.

One day he awoke knowing he had, during his sleep, been given a gift from Providence such as no man had ever received; a stroke of genius of unquestionably divine origin. He must work harder, but in a far profounder way than the believing shepherds. He would go beyond them, the monks and the New Testament. He would expand upon the prayer of obeisance by-may the reader understand the significance-multiplying by thousands the number of bows before the Highest he would do every day. He was asked, 'How is that prayer? You are only bowing repeatedly.' He answered 'No brother, the prayer lies in the bow, thus the greater number of those the holier the prayer'-the power of numbers made it holier. Here Simeon winked and admitted that he knew well enough that prayer was a matter of spirit, and that a bend or two did not equal a godly petition. But ten thousand bends! Such a vast sum had to amount to something. It is the gigantic numeral, then Simeon's eyes became fixed-I tell you it is meaningful, he insisted, for it is the high count that matters.

Simeon hesitated, gazing out upon the horizon for a moment, then continued. 'Note well, my biographer, how the daily mass of pilgrims is so great that I fear the foundation of my column will give way. Had I bowed at a certain time of the day the crowds would have been greater still and my column would surely have toppled, or you would have needed a royal escort to conduct your interviews. And if, in some, a deadly hysterical fit had been produced, what then? The masses would have grown to Biblical proportions. For it is just as true of rising popularity as it is of my endurance when we heed the command: 'Consider it pure joy, brothers, whenever you face trials of many kinds, because you know that the testing of your faith develops perseverance.'

I wrote that this was Simeon's equation of Truth, that a Christian pastor was one who accumulated a thousand million meaningless actions, and the megachurch was an equal number of those who were weak or not Christians, obtained by believing that the high figures have it.

When the biography was almost done, Simeon had me read it back to him. Since then he has refused to speak to me.

Successive crowds of pilgrims from Gaul and India saluted the divine pillar of Simeon: the tribes of Saracens disputed in arms the honor of his benediction; the queens of Arabia and Persia gratefully confessed his supernatural virtue; and the angelic Hermit was consulted by the younger Theodosius, in the most important concerns of the church and state. His remains were transported from the mountain of Telenissa, by a solemn procession of the patriarch, the master-general of the East, six bishops, twenty-one counts or tribunes, and six thousand soldiers; and Antioch revered his bones, as her glorious ornament and impregnable defense. (Penguin p. 430).

A Little Bit of This and a Little Bit of That vs. But She Out of her Poverty . . .

The community of goods . . . was adopted for a short time in the primitive church. The fervor of the first proselytes prompted them to sell those worldly possessions which they despised, to lay the price of them at the feet of the apostles, and to content themselves with receiving an equal share out of the general distribution . . . since the Jews, under a less perfect discipline, had been commanded to pay a tenth part of all they possessed . . . it would become the disciples of Christ to distinguish themselves by a superior degree of liberality and to acquire some merit by resigning a superfluous treasure . . . (p. 265 MLE).

Loiter among the church crowds and you will find there is a certain kind of religiosity that the people and especially the pastor-occasionally in his sermons but more regularly in his life-mock as unChristian. It is a religiosity that currently very few take up so it hardly carries any meaning for anyone, so it is a little odd that it should be brought up at all. But in centuries past it was more normative, a religiosity that gave up everything and sought out the lonely chambers of stone walls, far from the delights of the eye and the desires of one's heart.

The monks might indeed contend with the Stoics in the contempt of fortune, of pain, and of death and they disdained, as firmly as the Cynics themselves, all the forms and decencies of civil society. But [they] aspired to imitate a purer and more perfect model. They trod in the footsteps of the prophets, who had retired to the desert (p. 644 MLE) (italics mine).

This expression of Christianity is the butt of ridicule; it is seen as running away, escaping from the world, Christianly useless etc. Nowadays evangelical leaders have a far better grasp of what it is to give; by increasing their lot in life, to give a thousand out of a hundred thousand, to make more so as to give more, to shout out God's praises at the money for this, that, and the other.

How like the poor widow, who by giving her last and only penny could not hide it from an observant Jesus.

What a masterpiece of trickery these leaders take part in! To determine one's giving like this is to take God for a fool, for it is an easy copy of the profane. To do this is to bank one's hope entirely on mammon, that form of faith! This is alleged to be a higher form than the monks. But the advantages of such giving are concrete: to indulge in material comforts then call this trick Christian stewardship, a much more responsible use of God's gifts than the monks just handing their possessions over to the order and then retiring behind walls. If one were to convene the most cunning secular minds in history they could not have come up with such a plan for craftily weaseling money out of the pockets of the poor and Christian masses. The whole thing is a sickness unto death.

I am not advocating the monastery or the nunnery. I simply maintain that in the most spoiled church in history not only are we unable to do this ourselves-give our substance away for solitude-but few of us even know anyone who has ever done this. Of course Christ did not retreat permanently. What he did do is commend a widow for giving all she had; her hobbling along disguised the magnificent statement she had just made, that she was engaged in a battle with mammon; that this was being waged before an unbelieving age. No doubt the Pharisees heard what Jesus heard, the clank of the single penny in the treasury box over against the jingling of their many coins. Without a word, yes, in holy silence with eyes cast outwardly on the box but inwardly upon the object of her faith, she defies the age not behind the walls of a cloister but before the world. This is Christianity: to serve God in public, right before their eyes, to make such a clear assertion of faith a gaggle of witnesses would be eager to testify against her-why do you give when you are poor yourself? Watch, you will end up depending on us-this they cannot ignore. No evangelist of mammon would let this pass without a certain kind of ostracism. Give of your substance quietly and your act will be spoken of as an exaggeration. Speak out humbly for sacrificial giving and the persecution becomes more active. Twain's famous comment that 'there is nothing more irritating than a good example' is magnified considerably when that example starts talking. Once in Cairo I was walking in a neighborhood where several small boys, dirty and disheveled, thinking I was a tourist, accosted me for money. They accepted my refusal graciously. I realized later they were probably from the nearby City of the Dead-a cemetary where the living poor made their homes-and were looking after one another, giving up their widow's pennies for each other. Though disappointed, they responded with a sense of infinite resignation, which compounded my regret. The boys had become a Christian example, to give to one another and suffer for it.

What is the consequence for the Christianly obedient? A New Testament fact: that the more one gives of one's substance the more one comes into collision with the world and the conformed church. The world will think you are intoxicated, but ecclesiastics know well what you do and will make every conceivable attempt to ostracize, threaten, cajole, persuade, and by the use of religious language-O blessing!-entice you materially. They will point to themselves as examples of those who have sacrificed for the truth. This, in order to tempt you out of venturing.

When I say they will speak of their own sacrifice, it could very well be that they have, with enormous financial backing, established ministries in hard hit lands, then have sent various groups for short term stays. Wondrous servant leadership! To extend abroad what they have been doing at home-What sacrifice! How proud the poor widow would be! To make such a fabulous spectacle of yielding to the demand of the poor widow. Marvelous testimony! And because of this give-a-little-something attitude of the pastor/priests, those of us who have made it our lives to really give have to live down the caricatures of Christian giving that the pastor/priests have set up. They are like the wealthy father who neglects his children, putting on an ostentatious display of paternal care by purchasing expensive toys to appease his conscience and keep them quiet. It reminds of the monks of the fourth century, who according to the pagan Zosimus, had reduced a great part of mankind to a state of beggary. Except now we have the spiritual beggary of the West. These are the conformed church pastor/thieves. For love of Christian giving twenty thousand children die daily. Africa and India are what they are, with the additional seasoning that preachers use the twenty thousand as rhetorical devices to hone their speaking skills. Have no doubt then that these same evangelical leaders will use all the power of politics to protect and defend themselves, to maintain the entertainment of the circus at the expense of the people. This is precisely how it has been done in the past, and each time our nation's president will be the foremost guest in attendance.

And what the compromised pastoral authorities want from you is just the same as what the world wants, which is the same as the prince of this world, and that is to allow you to think that by giving something-a tenth-combined with your good intentions, you are serving Christianity.

Test yourself then to see if you follow the Master. Just as the Alaskan dog-sled driver examines himself to see that not one patch of flesh is exposed, and the camel driver covers his face as the Khamsin wind rolls off the Sahara, so are you to prepare yourself for who you serve. If you yourself are to recognize that you have been taught by the Galilean, and that you are with Him and long to be with Him, then this will be seen. How? By how much you cut into your gold, goods, and retirement fund so you could be free enough to serve the Master. Does your service in the house church and among the poor do irreparable harm to your career and make you less marketable to the world? Does it do away with your American dream and mine your possessions, only because of your love for the Master? These will be the Examiner's questions, and you may know just how near to Him you will stand by the evidence of your answers.

The interest of the pastor/priest: A young man of fine upbringing becomes enamoured of a girl in his church youth group, and, in the spring of their lives, they marry and gracefully grow old together. She is still seen with her hand in his, or in more peaceful moments her head on his shoulder, just as in the days of their youth. It is a singular matter then when one golden autumn evening, just as they whisper about the intensity of vermillion in the bright morning star, he takes his last breath, and she, unable to lift her head from his chest, prays: I am of all women most blessed, for I have seen Thy love through the love of this man, who has given me all a woman could ever dream of and such joy, for I remained the delight of his eye and the desire of his heart.

I know what other women say, that hope disappoints, and the hoped for. But this is the beauty of my sadness, that I never knew this disappointment, only what was higher, and that from my beloved.

Now, in truth, she will never know that had they, by the passion of a real Christian conviction, sold the soothing quiet that was the fulfillment of their dreams, he would have had to fight melancholy, resentment, and be a temptation to flee from! For an enclosing reserve would have enveloped him. No, she will never know this side of him, that had they ventured would have been an additional cross for her and for him as well. He simply never knew himself. Perhaps now we can hope she becomes that poor widow.

But who receives primary blame if she ventures little? Her pastor/priest, for he never confessed and gave as he was demanded to confess and give. Not once in an unexamined life did he ever venture to repeat in some fashion the candid confession of a Benedictine abbot: 'My vow of poverty has given me a hundred thousand crowns a year; my vow of obedience has raised me to the rank of a sovereign prince.' What is the major crime in this confession? Not that the abbot stole this money and principality, but that he considered owning it at all.

When I walk through my town in India I cannot avoid the idolmaker's shops. My thoughts always drift to the early church era where the clay idols were thought of as corporeal representatives of actual demons. The clay figure of Vesta was considered an authentic model of her in the spirit world. The same is true of mammon. I picture Tertullian in his censure of luxury perhaps saying 'The foreclosure on your home is a divine gift, a severe mercy. The chains of riches held by the ever-ravenous Mammon are to be replaced by a new yoke, a light burden where you will find rest for your soul.'

In connection with Tertullian's condemnation we are increasingly looking at a new breed of pastors who are leading the middle class megachurches, also known as the emerging church, headed by Jakes, Page, Warren, Hybels, and Hunter. These are said to be more serious about the whole counsel of God, i.e., they address the environment, human slavery and trafficking, prison reform, the death penalty, refugees, hunger, the Congo and sub-Saharan Africa, war and peace, the treatment of women, fair trade, AIDS as well as abortion. What they say about these matters are true, for the facts express it. However, a second question is then rightly asked, who is talking and what does their life look like. If it is the neighborhood gossip, a politician, the nouveau riche, a general, an arms dealer, weapons maker, or Wall Street banker who all say 'lay up for yourselves treasures in heaven,' then we know our speaker to be well-versed in literature but not serious about true religion. The same is true with our progressive pastors. When Christ said to 'watch,' He was not speaking only of His return, but to carefully note the expressions of the present age, such as the lives of the speakers and what they express. When, along with their costly edifices, middle class pastors lead middle class lives (flirting with luxury), mixing in an occasional trip to an inner city ministry or poor nation, who then say 'lay up treasures in heaven,' then something is up, the game is on, a ruse is being attempted. But when Christ says 'lay up treasures in heaven,' then our attention is riveted, for proofs are provided. The world's laughter and mockery begins when the word treasure is used by the progressives, for clearly some coin has spilled out of heaven's chest and into the laps of these fortunate. Yet there is nothing to joke about when the Giver enters the room and suddenly all is seriousness.

When He spoke of treasure He perhaps was thinking about the very natural, human desire for fame and fortune. We forget that the only One who ever gave every iota of His being (aware every second the more He says the more He provokes the clergy to take His life) to set all that aside and say 'I am glad to speak to you of what concerns you, treasures . . .' while living with the unspeakable sadness that even His beloved would reject Him, then to ignore this and remember us and our desire for fame, fortune, and treasures.

None of us enjoys forgetting earthly treasure. The secularist does not even think about forgetting mammon, the weak believer only would forget it to his secret horror. The pastor/priests act with the conceit that they are free to help themselves to the divine AND earthly treasures, and that they are entitled to it by their words. To give as the widow gave, this is worthy of a sermon certainly, but only as it relates to giving to the reverend's own church, something that Christ never said. But the pastor himself giving so much that it mimics the widow? Well thank you very much, but I would rather wait on the Lord's guidance for that. This is the primary problem for America's pastor/priests; this is what will determine if they will have faith or not. The more the stress is placed upon doing as the widow did, approximating this as close as possible, the smaller the authentic Christian church in America will be. When the example of the widow is made into a set percentage-the tithe-then the megachurch grows in leaps and bounds. If it is spiritualized (when giving becomes only a matter of good intentions, the hidden inwardness of a soaring heart meant for quiet times) then we should say a final Good Night to the widow's mite, for now every who in Whoville knows Christian sacrifice by just meaning well.

Yes, it could have been different; Christians over the centuries sought to redirect us by giving of their substance, of their own lives. But the sheer insolence of the conformed church right reverends meant increasingly cunning applications of Christian giving-in ways far worse than the Pharisees-until contemporary evangelicalism arrived with either no application or a minimal one at best.

Evangelical media (backed by concentrated finance-O if James had seen this!) makes the same claim that America does, that the U.S. is a Christian nation, that the founding fathers were Christian etc., therefore pagans in every land revile Christianity, which is not Christianity at all but the pastor/priest's self and group love. In every religious discussion I have ever had in a Muslim or Hindu land my own expression of Christian giving has never been ridiculed-no matter how weak or pathetic it was-but the offerings, or lack of, from the American churches have and with passionate hatred.

Anyone who has ever spent time in train stations in poor countries has seen the children. They may even grab you and you have to pry them loose. Once in Delhi's station I observed a little girl, perhaps seven, walking on the platform in what looked like dirty pajamas. She had a pretty face but it was filthy, and there was an open wound on her leg that she only pointed to when she went to beg from a traveller. When she was rebuffed, which was always, it was as if she had been slapped, and she would weave her way around the people, pillars and baggage, mumbling something to herself, sporadically scanning for foreigners. She was careful not to stray too far from the other child beggars nearby. The crowd, as it unceasingly does in such cases, treated her as an obstacle. To see this child's near frenzied sadness, face down, arms at once dragging in the hundred degree heat then up to beg, touching what could be touched, then repeating those actions was too much so I left my protected cafe to give her something. When I bent down to her level she was not looking at me, but when she turned around there I was and she jumped back. Yet she quickly took the money and asked for more, bending in Indian tradition to touch my shoes. I told her enough and returned to the cafe until my departure. She could not enter so she waited by the door, sometimes whistling to gain my attention. Two hours passed and she was still there, sitting, waiting. As my train pulled out I could see her resume her routine, looking up with hope then down with despair. Then I thought of the megachurch . . .

You see Christianity's view of this is very simple: to Him that little girl is not in the train station walking, begging, but in the American megachurch walking, begging, and people just keep treating her as an obstacle. Christ, with eyes of fire, light and sympathy fixes on her every insensible move as she makes her way around the stage, where Osteen is giving a sermon on how to incorporate giving into the family budget. There she is tugging at his pantleg, but nothing, no response. And Christ, who rises from His throne as He watches every little nuance of this child's agony, also hears the beginning of the sermon, when His name is invoked, and thus waits to see what is to be said and done with this little girl. Nothing, in fact, is done at all. But it turns out that much is said, for the more Osteen speaks the more his voice becomes choked with the tears he sheds at the suffering of the Indian children for lack of a sensible family budget! If it is a fact-and it is because He expressed it-that Christ did not hinder the children from coming to Him, then woe to Osteen and the megachurch pastors when Christ hears their sermons about not hindering the children from coming to Him. Indeed, each of us is to be held to a detailed account for every time we heard the story of Christ and the children and did little or nothing, particularly the clergy but the congregations too. For I would not put it past the shrewdness of the speakers, with their desperation for a large audience and greater fame, to point right at that little girl and ask, 'Will you let the children come to you or will you hinder them?' But remember that that little girl still shuffles around his pulpit, mumbling, waiting, making his hypocrisy far more abominable than that of his congregation's.

One more example-from Egypt. Church leaders have within the past fifteen years taken up the cause of central Africa. What Ruanda was, in its shocking horror, for a hundred days, central Africa has been for thirty years. There, victims are sliced, shot, and hunted into neighboring lands, with very little evangelic light shed on the matter until the international media began to take notice, then the pastors saw their chance and leaped in, at a distance of ten thousand miles, to broadcast the suffering of others. This, mixed with a few trips there to lend zest and piquancy to the appearance of giving. Yes, a trace of nutmeg here, a suggestion of clove there, and popular ministers take center stage in the fight for the life of the African poor. Therefore it is my task, with thanks to God that it was given me to not just become a part of the refugee church in Egypt for some years, but to make it known what Christians must do. Nothing of a revelatory nature has been disclosed to me, its all there in the New Testament. Yet it was for me to actually live there, then return to the U.S. for short periods to tell the pastor/priests what was as welcome to them as rat poison to rats. The notion that their defense of the African was an electrifying game was the first time these pastors had ever been confronted with their scam, which is why they scurried away. But the disease they carry has unleashed upon Christianity a pestilence infinitely worse than the plagues that ravaged Europe in the Middle Ages, for with these one only dies once, but the plague the pastors carry means the sickness unto death. These great men of God who dig the mass graves of the third world, preach long and often, perhaps even accompanied by a refugee, make a good salary (this from their storytelling, but to tell a story while actually living there is another matter) from the burning deaths and prolonged torture of poor Christians, but when it comes to selling their cars, fine homes, and well appointed church buildings, then moving there (so that their lives can begin to share a little of the suffering of the victim), they beg off at a huge distance. Yet before the widow at an infinite distance in the enjoyment of life.

Thus finding that poor neighborhood for one's house church is an attempt at taking on a shred of the marginalized Christian's agonies, or the suffering which would come from confronting the church leadership on the basis of its false concern for the maimed, the lame, the poor etc.

'What is Christianity saying, that we ought to work just

to give it all away?' No, Christianity does not say this. What it does demand is the purification of mind, body, and soul, perhaps slowly, nevertheless markedly, in a way that expresses Christianity.

Our esteemed reverends teach the contrary, that it is possible to pursue a career AND at the same time express Christianity by giving something to the church. This is the blasphemy that provokes God repeatedly. Instead of confessing that my well-salaried career is what has driven me, with giving a secondary concern, the two are merged as equally important, when giving and career are as different as a gold ring is to a pig's snout. A careerist moves away from the widow while professing a commitment to her faith and actions, which is ridiculous and hypocrisy.

Christianity moves toward the widow by taking a lesser job over the career, thus freeing one up to promulgate Christianity. The more time one spends doing this the more one gives out of one's living, because one has the time for those in need. This is a simple matter and the pastors know it because thay have taken an oath upon the New Testament, making them the basest criminals in the world, for not only have they allowed their own lives to be stolen away by profit but they preach assurance of salvation to those who do as they do. If it is this assurance you are looking for first confess, then see what you can do to express your confession. If it is the opposite tack you take, the pastor's assurances, then they are meaningless and a path to the abyss.

That mighty warrior of nonviolence, Gandhi, though not a Christian was in much closer fellowship with the lowly widow and her penny than our worldly ministers. Yet he would not have accepted the widow's motive as normative for himself or others and came right out and said it.

But his self-denial was evident enough, whereas the pastors kiss the ground the widow walks on only to trample upon her with their lives. I paraphrase Gandhi now: Leave evangelical leaders to the widow's mite. If that is too much, leave them to Paganism.

That Evangelical Leaders are Living as if Jesus Changed His Mind

They [the second Nicene Council] unanimously pronounced that the worship of images is agreeable to Scripture and reason, to the fathers and councils of the church . . . A monk had concluded a truce with the demon of fornication, on condition of interrupting his daily prayers to a picture that hung in his cell. His scruples prompted him to consult the abbot. 'Rather than abstain from adoring Christ and his Mother in their holy images, it would be better for you,' replied the casuist, 'to enter every brothel and visit every prostitute in the city.' (p. 882 MLE) (italics mine).

Imagine the New Testament to be entirely different than what it is, that just before Christ's ascension He reversed Himself, preaching a whole new gospel. He said that His newer gospel also would show who His followers were, who obeyed His new words, who sought to imitate His revised version; that one could identify them because they lived out the changes He Himself made; that one would know the new gospel's disciples by their actions.

Who are these people? What was it that He re-stated? What

are the effects of the new expressions of love by which we know them?

The clergy have now been commanded, under penalty of perdition, to make haste for the suburbs. And if their blessed financial advisors (with their financially fortuitous interpretation of the parable of the talents) fail them, to cry out in sackcloth and ashes for a middle class neighborhood, with at least two cars. It is the law of self/group love and big expenditures that matters now. The old law of suffering, self-denial, of either shedding one's blood for the Truth or coming within range of it (or confessing that one has not come within range of it), has passed away.

The new law: Spend time and lucre on technology-cars, computers, televisions, gadgets and social media. Remodel your homes, for it is commanded you receive market value for your property (cf. above financial advisors).

Play golf, get season tickets to sports venues and forget not to add a bit of spiritual seasoning to this by petitioning the Father for grace in the fellowship you share in these activities.

Arm yourself. In His name protect your home at any cost. If you feel a bit queasy about weapons in your house, this is understandable because you are not yet mature in faith. Trust God and the police, who are sufficiently equipped with the guns you paid for. Enjoy your personal security.

With respect to national security, the new Christianity has blessed us with another Christian President who, pursuing the peace, has blessedly prepared us for war. What protection from our enemies under the God-given umbrella of the nuclear triad, He, out of sacrificial love, has provided! With help from taxes, political support, and servants of Christ hard at work within the weapons industry, the old Jesus of Nazareth just looks like a godless fool compared to our comfort levels under the newer, more refined, Christ.

Now this version demands you work for the Good by joining a political party. The old version claims your party is nothing but a sugar-coated evil on a grand scale, that it works injustice in the name of justice like Capone running a charity as a front. Not so! Bank on the party to disciple Christians since it is Bible based. As America is gradually proselytized by means of the party, the more God is pleased.

By all means have at least a couple children, the Lord will provide and are we not told to do so in Genesis? Is it not a sign of God's favor? Do not tell your children they must endure four score years of pain (something the Old Testament also says), because you could not check your yearning to create after yourselves, that you could not exercise some self-control, all of which is, of course, the first version of the New Testament. No, teach your children as you were taught:

'Your coming into being was a miracle so commit your life into His hands. You were born into a land more fortunate than others so remember to give thanks daily. He will not give you everything you ask for but He will give you abundant life.' Then that clergyman sets the example of just what that means.

Make certain you are involved in a small group Bible study and that your children are in the youth group, for they too are to be instructed in the pastoral family's means of happiness (the joy of Christ is now annulled).

Avoid, a thousand times avoid what Bonhoeffer calls civic courage, especially if your standard of living would be reduced. Does the Father of all good things really want you to suffer? On two matters you may take a stand, abortion and gay marriage. In taking a stand on these two issues, you are absolutely safe from any Christian anguish that the older version would have you experience. Further, you will gain applause, pats on the back, and Lord willing, votes for any political aspirations you might have. Know IN YOUR HEART you will be identifying with Christ, yet the hosannas console you in your affliction.

Since Christianity has destined you for a family in the suburbs, for a church there, there will be no need for you to go where Christianity has not been heard, where it is a danger to be. There, where poverty is guaranteed and Christianity is purified as nowhere else, according to the old New Testament version. You may admire those who do but only at a distance and do not, do not speak with missionaries at length (unless you plan on lecturing them on the meaning of the second NT version). Do not question them in depth, read what they read, see what they see, or watch how awkward they seem around wealthy evangelicals. These missionaries do not appear to know what to say or do (except tell their own stories), a result, undoubtedly, of old version nonsense.

If you must go to the suffering abroad there are a number of things you can do to annul the long term effects. Embed yourself among other Americans or Westerners, preferably soldiers. If you meet missionaries, then a look-see is enough and be sure to take some photos, which will serve as proof back home of your suffering for the Truth. This is a critical part of trumpeting your visit (cf. Rick Warren, Ted Haggard, Franklin Graham). Do not remain quiet about any perceived good you may do (that is old version). You are a tourist now, a tourist of others' spiritual and material hunger, and this can mean a world of added credibility and prestige, or at the very least another building annex. Be sure to keep in touch with the State Department, to plan and protect yourself every step of the way.

These trips are honestly too risky for personal comfort and it is best to forego them altogether, for the first New Testament then has too many means to insinuate itself into your life on a permanent basis. Just have your quiet time at home daily and give thanks that your current lifestyle is God's plan for you and yours, and that will be enough.

Lastly, sit down after church on a Sunday afternoon and enjoy that pot roast so that you can take full advantage of the Sabbath. Then turn on the football game while the children play wholesome video games. The Lord has blessed.

No wonder Luther wrote somewhere that in the history of the church God often is more prone to hear the curses of the godless than the hallelujahs of the pious. It is the most dooming heresy of which evangelical leadership is responsible: taking Christianity and turning it into . . . self/ group love. The unfathomable hubris of the Grahams, Robertson, Warren, Beck, Brewer, Dobson, Jakes, Hunter, Osteen, et al is such dogged spiritlessness that if God were to choose between accepting the worship of it or Hinduism's bug-cum-god, He would take the bug worshiper-to make His words into putting on layers of yellow fat.

Under the reign of Anastasius, this popular frenzy [of circus games and the two parties] was inflamed by religious zeal . . . Every law, either human or divine, was trampled under foot, and as long as the [political] party was successful, its deluded followers appeared careless of private distress or public calamity . . . the support of a faction became necessary to every candidate for civil or ecclesiastical honors . . . the blues [party] were zealously devoted to the cause of orthodoxy (p. 710 MLE) (italics mine).

Christianity, Israel, and American Church Authorities

The descendants of Abraham were flattered by the opinion that they alone were the heirs of the covenant . . . Yet even in their fallen state [post 70 A.D.] the Jews, still asserting their lofty and exclusive privileges, shunned instead of courting the society of strangers. They still insisted with inflexible rigor on those parts of the law which it was in their power to practice (MLE p. 240-41) (italics mine).

What is it that determines religion, one that maintains its followers in their identity through the acute variations of history. Is it not the refusal to yield, especially when faced with severe opposition? Is it not a lasting character forged by an enduring belief? Take the Jews, who though crushed physically and politically, hurled by the false Christianity of one nation to the lawlessness of the next, by the life of a shared holy covenant, it is still the same prayers, the same longing of the Psalmist; it is 'how long O Lord,' it is the notion of the synagogue united in the 'Blessed are you, Adonai, our God, Ruler of the Universe . . . Is it not this that has held the Jews together over the millenia?

Neither the violence of Antiochus, nor the arts of Herod, nor the example of the circumjacent nations could ever persuade the Jews to associate with the institutions of Moses the elegant mythology of the Greeks . . . The mad attempt of Caligula to place his own statue in the temple of Jerusalem was defeated by the unanimous resolution of a people who dreaded death much less than such an idolatrous profanation (p. 238-39 MLE).

The warning of Samuel, building on the faithfulness of the prophets, was that if they chose a king like the other nations, then the effects of this obvious seduction would be felt and real.

Thus it is that the greater portion of Israel now is being led by a vengeful spirit, secularism on the order of the West, a military outpost that does America's bidding, where the prophetic religion of their ancestors is maintained only by the few. Israel has lost itself, and the evangelical pastor/ priests who profess their undying love for the Jews do actively support this terrible forfeiture of faith and hinder those who seek it.

As one who lived in Palestine/Israel I, like many others, have stood on the Mount of Olives overlooking Jerusalem and recalled Jesus' lament. But my own melancholy was of a different sort than most evangelicals; it was composed of a synagogue, a forest, a ring and a mushroom in a cold northern land.

The year before my move to Jerusalem I lived in the city of Konin, Poland, that at one time held a small yet thriving Jewish community. I often walked by the old synagogue and there someone gave me a book about the personal lives of the Jews who called that city their home before the Shoah. The

author's research made the neighborhood come alive again-
easy to picture when architecturally little had changed-and I
came to know these folk as if they were still there, the children,
personalities, routines, etc. Not a self-contained community,
there was much daily contact with the traditionally Catholic
Poles. It was a place of mutual toleration and respect. Then the
Holocaust. A large number of Konin's Jews were herded into
trucks and driven to a vale in a nearby forest. There they were
ordered to throw everything of value into a pile, before being
pushed into a hole that was to be their tomb. The line of victims
was so long that a man, or woman, managed to toss a wedding
ring through the trees without being seen.

A generation passed and mushroom pickers near the site
noticed a shining object and went to investigate. There, on top
of a mushroom, lay a gold ring.

As I looked down upon the Wailing Wall I thought of purity
rising out of the dirt and weeds.

Indeed if purity of heart, as has been said, is to will one thing,
then it was Christ's yearning that the gold ring, the Messiah of
the prophets, emerge glowing out of the stinking filth of Nazism.

A nation bound on revenge is no gold ring, and it is the
comfortable American pastor's secret desire to put a just and
prophetic Israel out of its misery. My first week in Palestine/
Israel was marked by an all-compelling desire to visit the Trappist
Monastery of Latroun, near the plain of Sharon in the foothills
that surround Jerusalem. This is because my sojourning friend
of many years, Kent Mathews, and I had come to the conclusion
earlier to travel separately and live in places of need around the

world, exchanging contacts as we moved, and he chose Latroun as his first stop. His journey ended later when he was hit on his bicycle by a drunk driver, while he was living among the handicapped in France.

I discussed his life with a monk there, who told me Kent had worked and conversed daily in the gardens with Palestinian Christians, who could only be there because they had special work permits to cross into Israel proper. While I waited for the bus to take me back to Jerusalem, I noticed a tank nearby with a sign that indicated an Israeli military museum a mile away. What a terrible-in the sense of the Absolute-judgmental irony! The same weaponry, bought with loving care with the taxes of Bible believers in America (the source of so much, so much misery for Palestinians), right there next to Kent, a very man of the Torah, who was there to demonstrate the meaning of the Old Testament to the chosen people. They might as well have set the iron machinery against the prophet Jeremiah for all the good it will do. No, all the armor that an evangelically led America and political Israel can possibly deploy will not avail against the faith of Kent Mathews. The well known picture of the Chinese student in Tiananmen Square blocking a line of tanks is as a gnat on the antler of a buck compared to one man surrounded on every side, one man who lives out his love for the God of Abraham, Isaac and Jacob, the God of Jesus Christ.

Dobson, Hagee, Osteen, Robertson, Coulter, Falwell, the Grahams, all those evangelical supremicists urging the government to arm Israel, they will in eternity be forced to view that one man against a trillion tons of metal.

Fret not though, our saintly pulpiteers still have America's eighty million and history's numerous Crusades they can use to justify their self-love in favor of a lethal, nuclear bloated Israel:

The Christians affirmed that their inalienable title to the promised land had been sealed by the blood of their divine Savior; it was their right and duty to rescue their inheritance from the unjust possessors . . . Vainly would it have been alleged . . . that the God of the Christians is not a local deity, and that the recovery of Bethlehem or Calvary, his cradle or his tomb, will not atone for the violation of the moral precepts of the gospel (p. 1052 MLE).

American ministers reluctantly admit that Israel has certainly made mistakes but the errors are excusable because that small nation is trying to survive amid a desert of hostile neighbors bent on pushing them into the sea. God gave this land to the chosen people, the Jews, and anyone who seeks to frustrate that purpose is fighting against God Himself. Biblical prophecy will bear that out and look what is happening now. So the argument goes. We will return to this.

O Jeremiah, if with noisy gong and clanging cymbal, if without tears you had preached the destruction of an insolent Israel, the priests would surely have conquered, accusing you of coldness and distance from the people. No, you spoke out and wept; you felt in your severity a wrenching sadness at what was about to occur to those whom you had given your life, making it clear that it was the king and the priests who were heartless.

But as it was demanded of you to speak through your sorrow, so you aroused the hatred of many by telling them they had become what they worshiped, worthless gods, thus they bore false witness against you and imprisoned you; the same is true now as it was then, that every Jew in Israel, every Palestinian or American who seeks to live out the meaning of the Torah, the prophetic, will be locked up or deported from the holy land. Jeremiah, you make it evident that a Jew is not a Jew by race or birth, but by a circumcised heart.

No manner of outward appearance can accomplish this, what the studious and stylized ultraorthodox should already know, if they only dared heed the Messiah on this.

I often rented a room near a nunnery in a Haredi neighborhood in Jerusalem where the streets would be blocked by garbage on Sabbaths so no cars could get through. There were many children outside-the orthodox generally have large families-who live in small apartments. It has always been a rather simple matter for me to speak with children. Simple because all one has to do is remember what it was like when one was a child. Not so here. I would greet the children whose faces I knew and saw daily, and they would only stare back at what they were told was the unclean gentile. The nuns said they themselves were occasionally spit on by the adults, as the nuns represent the man whose name it is forbidden to utter. But this behaviour could not have been taken from Abraham, who was just and friendly to the alien and stranger. Nor could it have come from Moses, the author of the Pentateuch (whom many orthodox hold to be the only divinely inspired writings), who himself had been an alien and sojourner in Egypt, a fact God repeatedly reminds Israel of.

Of course I was disappointed at the cold reception of my east

Jerusalem neighbors, for I had imagined myself arguing Torah with the elders. This reasoning was somewhat justified because I always had a give and take friendship with my Jewish childhood friends. We would go to synagogue and the Jewish Community Center, and I would question them about their Hebrew lessons after school. We would have brief but honest conversations about the differences in our faiths, and at the age of seven we were more straightforward than most adults, never attacking but always curious. At twenty two I visited my first concentration camp, Dachau. While waiting for a bus there, we stood outside for two hours, getting an idea of the frigid cold the prisoners had to endure. While living in Poland I was at Aushwitz-Birkenau twice, then once to the Warsaw Ghetto Memorial. In Jerusalem I boarded, every day, the same number buses that had earlier been turned into blazing coffins. I have spent time at Yad Vashem, the renowned Holocaust Museum, always by myself to be alone with my thoughts.

I was right to think, after traveling days to memorials, reading hundreds of letters, examining the facial expressions on thousands of pictures, writing down quotes, studying books, defending the Jews in cafes and classes in the Middle East, Poland, and India, scoffing at conspiracy theories, taking Augustine to task (he wrote the Jews should be scattered)-yes, it was my thought that the orthodox would want to speak with the gentile traveler 'who loves our people,' if only because I greeted their children. That chance was denied (unless you pay money for it), and the tradition of the Pharisees lives on.

Discussions were carried on anyway; a group of waitresses

who passionately and quite wrongly claimed there was nothing in Christian history that exemplified toleration toward the Jews. Yet the only reason they were speaking to me at all was that I was teaching Palestinian children in a forsaken city, something they had a little sympathy for.

So when I say from the standpoint of the Torah the majority of Israel is faithless, I am not just another blowhard from a radical cocoon, for I have done more to grasp Israel and its history than any of these so-called friends of Israel have. These cowardly whiners in soft clothing and beautified churches who love Israel so much that-now reader steel yourself-they vote pro-Israel. Pose a challenge, my reader, dare to test this great defender of Israel (who stands behind his pulpit), and ask him to visit a Palestinian school in the West Bank and THERE defend Israel's right of existence-which I did repeatedly-among the students. Then see the Reverend-Great-Defender-of-Israel smile, nervously equivocate and stammer out that this is not God's will for his life etc.

Note too how these same pastors (who run so much from danger they really ought to travel to Australia to observe how rabbits scatter en masse) are the same ones who are the loudest against abortion and gay rights, two concerns that imply such enormous peril for their lives. Be absolutely certain that if the Jews were to enter again into the cattle trains of a new Shoah, conformed church leaders would stand as flatfootedly stupid and silent as they did in the mid 1930s, when American covert operations in Europe discovered the intent of the Nazis, and the world press was covering events such as Kristallnacht. Fact:

John Morton

Evangelical authorities closed the door to Jewish refugees, thus placing their blood on the doors of the churches, a sort of Passover in reverse.

And what were these authorities doing? Too busy preaching against alcohol to pay any notice. Besides, it might dilute the pure gospel if they were to snatch the Jews from the jaws of death.

This is why the scriptures place the majority of America's pastor/priests in the same spiritless position as the majority of a political Israel. And on the contrary the small minority of pastor/ priests who seek to become New Testament Christians are at the same point of faith as the Jew who seeks the anointed One of the law and the prophets.

Now exactly why is the majority of Israel spiritless? The material point: It is because their confession-of those who confess at all in a largely secular Israel-is an abomination without obedience to Torah, something that the pastor/priests have a little experience of. It is the same old thing, reiterated about ten thousand times in the Old Testament (and what the rabbis and pastors endlessly reinterpret or reject), that God demands obedience before sacrifice, that Israel cannot keep repeating its love for Adonai without following His prominent commandments, made clear by the examples of Abraham, Moses, the patriarchs, David and the prophets. To be a Jew is not to play the role of Ahab and Jezebel, murdering Naboth then stealing his land as did the Israelis who, like mafia thugs, took the land of Palestinian farmers-who, again like Naboth, had had it in their families for centuries-giving nothing back but threats in 1948.

To be a Jew is not to destroy villages, as Israel did to Al Khaesah, Deeryassen, Al Ramlah and Ikret (there were more), spitting in the face of Isaiah, who chose to loose the bonds of wickedness; to not throw righteousness to the ground (Amos) and assault a Turkish aid convoy and accumulate bloodguilt. To be a Jew is not to torture, which I overheard even Israeli schoolgirls justify ('How else are you going to get the information?'), massacre (two hundred and fifty at Tantura) and establish places of grieving homeless by demolishing three thousand homes in the past 20 years, challenging Joshua, who read the law to both Jews and aliens living among them (this on the Samaritan mountain I lived on, Gerazim, in Nablus). To be a Jew is not to perform atrocities, such as blowing to pieces school children and handicapped in Gaza. To be a Jew is to not to permit, as Sharon did, the gunning down of refugees in the Sabra and Shatila camps, putting Moses to the test again, by mocking his cities of refuge. It is not to steal others' water, telling Solomon his proverb about using water only from your own well is not good enough when you with your Uzi have established a settlement on somebody else's land and you need their water. It is not to force natives of their own land to stand in line for hours to receive permits to move around in what is already theirs, or to wait at multiple checkpoints to go to work, school etc. in the place where their ancestors lived, which is showing the backside to Ezekiel, who demanded aliens be made citizens, with all the rights and privileges thereof, effective immediately. Thus a political Israel calls Abraham a liar, who practically forces justice upon Ephron (who was not a follower of the covenant), who greatly desired to gift Abraham with a cave for Sarah's burial, but Abraham refused and paid for it. It is not to deny aliens the right to work, students the opportunity to go to school and withold money (due Palestinians), putting to the sword every moral precept of law, history and major and minor prophet in the Old Testament. It is not as a nation of men to own above a hundred thermonuclear arms, deny it, then imprison Mordecai Vanunu (a Christian), for eighteen years, who was honest enough to admit he worked in this diabolical program, thus indicating to Adonai it was never His land to begin with (as Torah unquestionably makes clear), but the Jews to consider wiping from the map, all in revenge. To be a Jew is not to accept bloodmoney from preaching or prophecy heretics who claim kinship with the Jews, but really are addicted to fame (Lahaye and Jenkins come to mind), who make of Torah a board game for guessing the future and Adonai a player in THEIR game. This is money owed to the poor, but instead is given to a worse than apartheid government (apartheid in South Africa, for all its evils, did not slaughter eleven hundred children in one campaign as in Gaza). It is not to provoke the hatred the Muslim already sees for the Jew in the Koran, bringing to the surface a latent hostility (this replaced Arabic hospitality and tradition), making the Arabic Christian cry out to the Messiah for the remnant Israel of the prophets. Finally to be a Jew is to play the man, like David before Nathan, to say to Adonai this is what I have done, Thou knowest, now this is what I will do, and do it. Not to repeat 'national security' (which according to their own internal documents is not related to security but to standard of living) like a parrot, for the consistent excuse of a political Israel is the same as evangelical leaders, which is the same as the Torah faithless, that 'mistakes' have been made. The connotation is comical: 'O Magoo, you've done it again.'

Israel has the divine sanction to do these things because they are the chosen people, led by Joshua to cleanse the land of foreigners, or so goes much-but not all-of Jewish thinking. Nearly all of evangelical clergy's response to Israel grows out of this misinterpretation of the Old Testament.

But Joshua only eliminates those kings he is commanded to, those who resist him. He does not just take what he wants, like political Israel, but goes after kings who coalesce against him, and he represents Adonai. Only those. Moses had told him to attack followers of the Canaanite religion, a religion of child sacrifice and cult prostitution, with prayers to snakes. In that age-according to Adonai-this religion had to be placed under the ban. But those who chose life Joshua spares, like Rahab or the Gibeonites.

Continue with Joshua's life and you learn what he did and did not do in relation to Adonai's command. Only those most aggressive toward the Israelites were utterly destroyed; but the Galilee, Lebanon's coast and the hill country of Ephraim were left alone. Adonai takes issue with Joshua for not completing the task, but does not (the lightening judgment against contemporary Israel falls here) reissue the command to eliminate the Canaanites for the obvious reason that some had become followers of the God of Israel; one may add here that there are now many humble Muslims of which one may have a conversation on what God requires-not to mention the large number of Christians among the former Canaanites.

The standards of Joshua's day slowly began to change, with the prophets as the instruments of change. There is clear movement. The chosen people were told to act like chosen people. Their example would suffice for the unbelievers, bringing all nations under the Covenant. With the appearance of the Messiah, there was enough in the Torah to prepare them for Him, as Simeon, for one, knew. If not, if they chose to despise the sweetness of the law and stoned the prophets, the land would vomit them out.

This has begun, which is why the confiscation of Palestinian land continues and water is reason to war. The claim that Israel made the desert bloom is an empty boast, for all one has to do is add water-except for the arid east and south-and it becomes a land of milk and honey. Nevertheless resources are disappearing and creation care is of little matter. The young are reforesting but there is little they can do in a small, highly militarized, unrestrained materialistic culture with American-like avarice driving the economy. What Israel has done to Palestinian land is worse-building a monstrous wall, blowing up roads, scorched earth policies, stealing olives from olive groves etc. To be fair urban Palestinians have laid waste their own cities and roadsides, though one could hardly blame Palestinian camp refugees that sewage runs down their gullies.

A rogue Israel desperate to maintain itself with more water and land will do exactly what it has done in the past-and what Adonai condemns every time-run begging to false friends for help as they did with Egypt when the Assyrians threatened.

Read where that got them. Israel thinks that by becoming a smaller, more well-armed version of its mentor that the U.S. will come to their rescue if an emergency arises, or that evangelicals will pressure the U.S. government to step up in a state of war. Since evangelical pastors ALWAYS initially support violence done in the name of freedom of religion, and since the crystal ball prophecies of Christendom have whipped up expectations for the second coming to near frenzy pitch (particularly during Sunday services) with their sacreligious predictions, it could very well come to pass that an atomically equipped Israel (along with its neighbors) just disappears under the dust of the Negev. If so, it will be buried with all the wishdreams of the end times quacks.

Small wonder some Israelis who know their history and theology warn their government not to make common cause with nincompoops like Hagee, LaHaye, Jenkins etc. whom they know to be self-lovingly so obsessed with their group's rapture that they are prepared to sacrifice the whole Middle East to their own ends.

Under the reign of Constantine . . . The civil immunities granted or confirmed by Severus were gradually replaced by the Chritian princes; and a rash tumult, excited by the Jews of Palestine, seemed to justify the lucrative modes of oppression which were invented by the bishops and eunochs of the court of Constantius (p. 447 MLE).

Meanwhile, do not ask the clergy to sell any of its fabulous properties to assist an Israeli economy when it hits its own wall of finite resources, for the church will continue to give off the top as it does with everything else. It cannot be that Israel has even a sliver of a chance of survival unless it begins to act prophetically, and that is to immediately implement the two state solution.

International law, which political Israel refuses to abide by (with U.S. support), has already set the boundaries. Let a stiff-necked political Israel repent itself by adhering to the boundaries.

The final move is to institute what the Jewish theologian Martin Buber called the Brit Shalom, the single state solution, with full respect given to the two cultures-as in India with Islam and Hinduism-thus the dismantling of the current apartheid state. If this happens, Israel deflates Hamas' push-Israel-into-the-sea movement and the majority of Muslims (because the foremost insult, the occupation, has been removed) cannot resort to the Koran as much to justify their hatred of Israel. There is never a guarantee of reconciliation, as the Old Testament prophets testify, but peacemakers have one thing on their side, be they searching Muslim, Jew or Christian, and that is eternal character, which is a far better companion before God than national security. Let religious sophists whine, moan, and wing their end times speculation around as much as they like; they do not have to live with the high anxiety for their safety as Israelis do. For the Christian it is enough to know that the conformed church pastors and a political Israel will diminish, while Christians and prophetic Jews maintain their hold on Joseph's dream.

The very same accusations will be flung against you, Christian, that were heaped on the prophets, of being anti-semitic, and against you, O Jewish, of being a self-hater or committing 'national suicide.' But out of the depths of the Psalms where peace and justice have kissed will come fair words in long dark nights. Indeed, you will have much to say and hear, when you depart with the Pauline-like blessing from your house church in America for Palestine/Israel, bringing back gold rings stolen from both groups. These gold rings have been refined by fire and will not fade away: the Law and the Prophets, the New Testament, a circumcised heart, time and money for the Palestinian church and those Jews who have no experience of the promised land. It will perhaps be the first time for both groups that they will have met a credible representative of the Prince of peace.

How Dare You Judge Us!

The martial youths [of the crusades] were fired by the reproach or
suspicion of cowardice; the opportunity of visiting with an army the
sepulcher of Christ was embraced by the old and the infirm, by women
and children, who consulted rather their zeal than their strength; and
those who in the evening had derided the folly of their companions were
the most eager the ensuing day to tread in their footsteps (p. 1056 MLE)
(italics mine).

'You would judge us? You don't even know us! You believe
we should be ashamed of our faith and our leadership? You
would demonize us? Who are you to tell us what the New
Testament teaches? Don't you think we care about the poor? We
have shown to have a real heart for the homeless. Are you even
aware of our ministries? You haven't even visited us. Proud and
vain man, it is you that needs to repent.'

If I may ask for only a moment of the reader's time, and a
little patience, I dare to explain.

The Christian must judge behavior-his own first. He allows
God to determine the reckoning, so he must examine himself
to discover where he errs, where he can yield more to God and

the one who seeks his help. He judges actions-his own first. He rejects usurping God's judgment. On the contrary, it is false Christian leadership that eternally judges the sincere Christian, indicating who it serves by how it treats him, like the King's court who laughed at the jester who warned of a rebellion brewing.

When Luther wrote that the lightening of God's wrath first strikes the churches, he was making a judgment echoing Christ's command to judge with righteous judgment. That is clear enough.

What is not always clear is that the word judgment is ambiguous. Of course the Christian never assumes the role of the Ultimate Determiner, for he can only surmise based on what he sees. Yet he sees with an eye toward judging himself first, then the behavior of the church, especially its leadership and authority. It discerns spirits, right and wrong, good and evil, then acts accordingly. This is Christ again and again. Simply, the New Testament requires the Christian to reject, withdraw from and excommunicate those whose lives have been nothing but a 'trial by water,' the play-actors of Christianity; this is an ethical/religious judgment of love.

My readers, why does this trouble you so? Certainly because, like myself, since our earliest days of Sunday School up through our impressionable youth we have had it drummed into our heads that the gentle Jesus of the paintings-however else He looked, He did not look like this-would not wisecrack, mock, physically disrupt the church (temple), harshly judge stupidity, harangue and use the pastoral class as an example of what not to be. Yet this is exactly what he did.

Then, to disabuse us of the notion that he was really a fine fellow, He claimed He would bring fire on earth, to divide, divide, divide.

There is a real honest-to-goodness religiously based judgment within the family. This family member against that family member etc. We must not only take his angry words as Christian against unbeliever, for recall that he spoke primarily before believing Jews. What He in fact addressed was true religion against false, straw versus gold, hollow versus solid, follower versus speechmaker-all Christian shadowboxing. For us this requires mature value judgments, and it is ordered we make them, for evidence of faith is demanded.

So what is to be done with this matter of eternal judgment? An example: Let us take a military man, a major, dedicated to defending the weak against the depradations of the strong, of sacrificing his life if necessary to protect a child. In this he is sincere. Blessed by the chaplain and his pastor at home, he is greatly assured he is fulfilling the divine plan for his life. Then, his unit is dispatched to an area of heavy fighting, where children are drugged into becoming butchers and rape is used as a means to terrorize the population. In a village he meets a missionary whom he respects, so the major offers him an embedment within the unit. The missionary kindly yet firmly refuses, telling the major that living Christianly is living dangerously, to put oneself at risk and in harm's way, since it is the only way the enemy can see true Christianity, that he is willing to lay down his life without taking one in return. The major gazes at the missionary, anxiously grasping the implication, with subjective effect. Well then, he asks, what do you think of me? It seems you reject my work as a Christian. Am I to be severely judged because I have killed defensively? The missionary in turn respects the major, knows his soul is at stake now. 'Friend, as a pastor I must tell you without hesitation-because the truth does not hesitate-that killing is Christianly forbidden and if you are to follow Him you must lay down your weapon. Major, sheathe your sword and join us here in a common work for Christianity.'

That, or something to that effect (and a lot of thanks I will get here for loving military evangelicals).

But the judgmentally challenged pastor/priests say something else. They offer up the necks of others for the sake of prestige, profit, and higher membership roles, opening wide their arms to say 'all are welcome as we prepare our hearts for worship.' This is why the President, who at that moment has made an appointment with the angel of death for who knows how many victims, can with clear conscience plop himself down in the pew then proceed to take communion. O what an accounting awaits those who make such a fool's game of the Lord's supper! Communion!

Where Christ presented Himself as the Sacrifice before His followers, all but one of whom were to imitate Him in being spit on, scoffed at, hated even as they denied themselves. They were prepared to be martyrs and blood witnesses. Now the President also becomes a blood witness to the Truth. So let us ask American church leadership: Why stop there? Why not give communion to the goose and the goat who led the procession in the first medieval crusade? At least the goat and goose have nothing to do with drone attacks on suspects and ordinary folk. But to deny him communion? God forbid say these bold men of God, for that would be judging him.

The vileness being played out is this: that the local abortion doctor could stand, unrepented, and take part in the same blood covenant as the apostles, and the pastors (made stupid by the praise of men) would never know it. No doubt even if the pastors did know their tears would flow as they admonished an equally moved congregation to judge not lest they be judged. Then communion is given to all.

Be it known that God is no friend of indolence, much less cowardice. He takes very seriously that they hide their obligation to make disciplinary judgments upon themselves first, then the church, which they do for a number of reasons: cash considerations, fine buildings, shining careers, visits to the White House, political influence, suits, robes, TV, radio, and news interviews-all this hangs together because the masses permit themselves to be deluded by sense impressions.

This delusion must go.

Right judgment is to force this matter of honesty: that I would rather sell slaves on the streets of Khartoum, be a polygamist, a male prostitute, steal from the wretched, than share in painting God's face as a clown; while my time away at the casinos and bars of Las Vegas than take a lifelong plunge into pastoral popularity in America.

I beg you, do not withold your imagination from this scene. The pastor, this soft clothed gentleman responsible for having led so many people astray, is standing before God pleading his case.

How will God hear it? He will look down upon this man as Pikes Peak looks down upon Colorado Springs. The pastor, whose entire life has been one of fraud, game playing, and deception, naturally will not have the courage to say, this is what I did; I am man enough to own it; I'll take what is coming to me. He will hem and haw and but, but, but until he is dispatched. Never once, as he looked into the mirror, did he examine/judge himself harshly enough to do an about-face, or at the very least be a little honest about the situation.

Karl Barth once said you do theology with a newspaper in one hand and a Bible in the other. It is the same with looking in the mirror. One carries the Word in his mind and spirit as he looks at himself. The pastor/priests know better than anyone what is in that Word (God has elected the base things of the world and the things that are despised; Put your sword back into its place; Now listen you rich people, weep and wail; If anyone has the world's goods and sees his brother in need, yet closes his heart against him, how can God's love abide in him?; Invite the stranger [illegal immigrant, foreigner] into your home; Peacemakers, who sow in peace, reap a harvest of justice; etc.). So sly are these leaders that first they paint over their mirrors with a hundred coats: the colors of money, country, a following, splendid surroundings, and critically, cherry picking their way though the Bible, all of which are expensive and enhance their self-assertion; these (the large buildings, their good salaries) they say are tools for Christianity, but are they not just more coats that make seeing and judging well nigh impossible? Christianity is precisely to strip away the accumulated layers so as to see clearly and judge rightly. It is to work backward to get to where one finally says; 'Aha, you!' Now one can move on to reckon the church's behavior accurately, for he gasped when he saw through a pinprick hole in the mirror, that while he thought he recognized others he had not recognized himself.

Pastors Dimm, Fog, and Blur have made salutary efforts at turning their mirrors into masterpieces, as their steady salaries indicate. With brush in hand, they stand a few feet back then describe the mirror as if it were at auction. This is what it is to make incomplete judgments or no judgments at all. Just as Christ asked his disciples that upon His return would He find faith on earth, this plaintive sigh also meant finding those who saw clearly, judged rightly. Dimm, Fog, and Blur honestly believe they are looking at themselves in their jaded looking-glass. This is the stuff of comedy if it were not for the Eternal. When a class moans and whines at the return of its strict teacher, it is easy to see they are of no mind to do the work the teacher imposes. Yet student Hobnoggin hits upon the idea that he will play up to the teacher, flatter, pretend he is overjoyed at his return, ever eager and earnest to get back to work. When the assignments come due the teacher realizes that Hobnoggin sitting in the front row, all smiles and politeness, has not turned one in. The teacher gives him a stern warning. With the gratitude that would shame a dog after the return of his long lost master, he tears up before his teacher and promises to rush home and do the work. Instead, he takes up with his companions at games all afternoon. Now do you think the teacher will put up with Hobnoggin's hearty welcome come grade time?, who perpetually erased the board and professed his respect for the teacher-just to get expelled.

Why the Christian is Happier, but Evangelical Leaders are the Enemies of Happiness

When the promise of eternal happiness was proposed to mankind on condition of adopting the faith and of observing the precepts of the gospel, it is no wonder that so advantageous an offer should have been accepted by great numbers of every religion, of every rank, and of every province in the Roman Empire. The ancient Christians were animated by a contempt for their present existence, and by a just confidence of immortality, of which the doubtful and imperfect faith of modern ages cannot give us any adequate notion (p. 251 MLE).

Sit down with an American cleric and a Palestinian pastor in the West Bank of Palestine/Israel and listen as they speak of Christianity and you will find no difference when they talk of faith as an absolute dependence on Christ, that such faith resides in the authority of the Teacher, that God came to earth (and lived in the West Bank) through a particular human being two thousand years ago etc. But this is where the agreement ends, for the Palestinian, Bishara, points out in the Bible that Christianity is more than this, more than just putting forward who Jesus is, more than just affirming His being, more than just spreading awareness of His nature. More than this. Here, our cleric, Dr. Mark, says of course Christianity is more than this (he even pointed this out to Pat Robertson), much more; that we must obey the Teacher by fighting abortion, homosexuality, sexual promiscuity, for family values (was he not known for being the Republican pastor?), and in this way turn cities like Los Angeles, his own, into cities of God. Bishara sighs and interrupts-otherwise he would not get a word in-claiming his congregation is now caught between Islamists and a political Israel blind to the law and the prophets, that neither he nor his flock have time to waste delving into doctrinal matters that have already been resolved; that for them becoming Christians is what is important, that Christianity is a way of life.

. . . *[Emperor Justinian] unknown to the [military] camp, was content to vanquish at the head of a synod. Had he invited to these synods a disinterested and rational spectator, Justinian might have learned 'That religious controversy is the offspring of arrogance and folly; THAT true piety is most laudably expressed by silence and submission; THAT man, ignorant of his own nature, should not presume to scrutinize the nature of his God; and THAT it is sufficient for us to know that power and benevolence are the perfect attributes of the Deity' (p. 835 MLE) (italics mine).*

Then he looks at Dr. Mark, asking gently yet firmly 'How is it that you Americans do this with the Holy Writings, that you pick and choose what you battle for in the Bible and neglect others?'

Those of you who have not only read holy writ but have immersed yourselves in it, is there not a sympathetic tug toward our Palestinian friend, who in his earnestness attempts to persuade the sheltered American, from his own life, the truth of the whole council of God?

In academic circles you will find many who know what it is to be a Christian without being one. Jog down I-83 in Colorado Springs to Dobson's Focus, past Haggard's old haunt, the colossal New Life complex, then head west a few miles to the Air Force chapel (the civil religion tour) and speak with clergy and laity at each place, whose New Testament knowledge is precise and exact, then see if you can find Christians among them. My point: Is there Christian faith in that man or woman? What an eternal travesty when with the help of the evangelical pastorate you find believers who have not yet become Christians.

I have maintained that most of America's pastor/priests use a cunning religious ruse for self-assertion and avarice, and if that is the case then the cruelest of all games is being played, and to the extent one plays it one becomes unhappy for this life.

When Augustine wrote that one's heart is not at rest until it finds its rest in God, he was thinking of a certain type of individual at peace, perhaps his beloved mother. Very far from this conviction were the swarms of worldly monks, absorbed as they were by the senses, things, which the blessed minister is always absorbed by, as if that is of any everlasting value. It looks to what this person does or that person, this person's tastes or that person's, not giving a whit for the 'Thou shalt,' and thus there is no measure of what one is to become, what is left behind and what is to be taken on. By not yielding to the eternal, but by embracing the perishable, not having the identity the spirit gives, having become just another man in the crowd, yet longing to be heard, he knows he is just another tie on a railroad track that ends . . . There is no better definition of a man without a country than the despairing unhappiness that comes with not becoming what one was meant to be. To perpetually fight off what one is pulled toward, of acknowledging with one's lips what is actively denied in one's life.

How profoundly unhappy most American ecclesiastics are, in ways that approach the intensity of despair, the unhappiness of the demonic (approaching, not demonizing). Outwardly, they may appear humorous to the unbeliever's eyes, but the old men of God, the Simeons of the land, know what it all means when the pastor weeps with bitter tears and storms across the stage, Bible in hand. There he declaims on bearing one's cross, the Sacrifice, how he himself would gladly lay down his life etc.-and then, after he wipes his face with a handkerchief he collects himself-makes a comical remark to relieve the tension-and immediately sets out to reaffirm conformity to the American dream. Perhaps, in the full bloom of youth, he felt a pang in his conscience that he was losing his enthusiasm, the contentment he felt in the spring of his conversion was no longer there, that he was digging a grave for the self that was meant to be, that Christianity was slowly withdrawing from him. But when he confronted his conscience with the lives of his rich and famous pastoral colleagues, the war was lost. He learned to buffet his conscience and make it his slave, so as to suffocate the despair of unhappiness that lurked beneath. And now look at him, with truth ringing out in his voice and his body sweating, poetically and passionately flailing away at all the principalities and powers, unwaveringly the Christian soldier, staring down evil, with no hesitation in his steps he stomps on the very gates of perdition. It is the unhappiness that runs in a circle that in the very next moment, while the sweat is still on his brow, he effeminately cringes and buckles under the slightest worldly seduction. What a wrenching unhappiness of impending doom dwells in the inner clefts of the man's heart, for indeed Osteen and his horde of sabotage artists are like men standing with each foot chained to two boats floating on the ocean, awaiting the seven miles below. However comical they may be cutting such figures, however much in my youth I enjoyed mimicking their monkey antics, now I find no pleasure in it. It is even possible to sorrow unto death over the masses, to watch as a pack of men in suits serve as Pied Pipers to those who succomb to their own weakness.

But suburban evangelicals, their triviality mixed with Bible studies and prayer meetings, suffer an unhappiness to a somewhat lesser degree since their guilt is not as great, though they too are guilty.

Again, after the initial joy of conversion wears off our suburbanite recognizes inwardly he is moving backwards, but needs the mega-numbers to convince himself he is moving forwards, yet he grows increasingly spiritless, thus unhappier. Though he is polite and civil, he lacks spirit because his life is nothing but what is expected; he rules out divine breakthroughs. Despite all his praises and hallelujahs, he fixes his life in such a way that it lacks possibility, which is necessary for developing as a Christian. Unreflectively he draws Christianity into the corral of triviality he himself lives in, the life of immediacy, pettiness, slight dreams outside of what is material, no matter whether he is an engineer for Raytheon or she is a homemaker, no matter if they attend a Bible study and home school their children or not. The slow disintegration of a life that was meant to be, hence the loss of Christianity happens when a man willfully exchanges the meaningful for the trivial, which is the typical suburban life.

To acknowledge the Spirit's ascendancy is to first dream New Testament dreams, then to take that dream and drive it hard at one's previous expectations, and the more one attacks them the more one dreams, for now the circle is broken and happiness increases because hope has increased. Dreaming Christianly is what the suburban evangelical finds very nearly impossible, and when those dreams are hinted at they are rejected out of hand with the stock phrase 'What can I do?' And when God permits some personal disaster to occur-car accident, illness, loss of job-then the evangelical, instead of taking it as an indication that a character action is in order, sees it as a trial and tribulation, something that must be endured until life returns to normal; a dream is lost along with its God, the despair of unhappiness intensifies and that person is lost for eternity.

Occasionally the unhappiness of that man, woman, or youth-locked into a frivolous family and seeing no way out-is so great that it bursts through the madhouse designed to keep it in. If one survives the force of the burst, there is now more hope because the walls have tumbled. I once worked as a counselor in a hospital where I spoke with a middle-aged woman (the wife of a suburban pastor) who had attempted suicide. She asked me what I did and I told her of our house church. Her response was immediate, that I not pray for her. I understood and said nothing, but did listen to the outpouring of bitterness that comes from living trivially for so long, of having to play a role she was not meant to play. I did not attempt to explain the situation, but she explained it to herself. Later I realized what I had witnessed was righteous indignation (felt by eighty million people in this land with a thousandth of them admitting to it) the resentment of being betrayed by the lies of their leader, the sound and fury of having a self snatched away. In any event she was unsure what to do with her anger, where to take it. The focus moved from the betrayal to the path out of it, of losing her trivial self and finding herself. Perhaps she did eventually escape the trap laid for her. Perhaps not. Yet with each drop of poison that spilled out of her there appeared a corresponding lift from a self long buried.

When it is said to evangelicals and their pastor/priests that with God all things are possible, that they are capable of doing more, much more, they nod in agreement (having grown up hearing this every day) but point to some circumstance that hinders them from taking greater risks. Even the day-to-day tedium of an unhappier life is not as horrifying as the thought of venturing in faith and failing miserably, perhaps having a nervous breakdown. Yet imagine a family that ventures anyway, moving with some kindred venturers into that so-called bad neighborhood to be the church there. Then their worst nightmare is realized, say gunshots are heard in the night. A despair such has never been felt before attacks every fiber of their faith, to where the family accuses the Lord Himself with the I-told-you-so of the despair of having risked everything and lost. For them it is the Abrahamic second just before the Voice is heard and the ram appears. What happens next is the miracle in the full New Testament sense-the hope that stays the course. The family revives.

In our house church some time ago a couple of newly-weds were planning a move onto our block and were set to go. The very night before their move their rental was destroyed by arson.

The couple questioned whether the divine No had been laid down. Immediately we met and sacrifices were made to accommodate the couple. The heartbeat of despair, the shortened breath of the sorrowful was gone as quickly as it had come.

My reader, Christianity itself will help you in the demanded renunciation of leaving the unhappy triviality of the suburban or middle class for the meaningful, happier life of Christianity among the poor. The horrors you imagine, Providence will either guide you around them or through them, as you thrive in the promised joy. But know that you will meet with the opposition of most of your believing friends, and you will find out from others just what they think.

You may receive their polite admiration, which is just another expression for their opposition, for in the quiet of their bedrooms they claim they could never do such a thing, how Dr. Dobson does not recommend it, how it is mad, impractical or unChristian to put your family at risk. Finally there is the stinging remark that puts an end to any thought of the imitation of Christ, that it may be fine for others but they are prevented from doing it because-and here is where the hailstorm of excuses begin. This, without giving five minutes to pondering where they might find assistance.

Then later they prattle on about how their good intentions were stymied by family or job obligations. O to what depths of unhappiness, of lies and self-deception can our oratorically gifted clergy sink!

One is reminded of the Roman philosophers who, in order to understand the voluntary sufferings of the early Christians, put it down to stubborness, despair, stupidity or fanatical hysteria.

Picture this: The President's prayer breakfast, with America's top pastor/priests present, is interrupted by some first century Christians who manage to disrupt the display. Arrested, they are brought before the court, demanding the judge inflicts the full sentence of the law. The judge is very cautious because American constitutional law makes no provision for such behavior. Charges are withdrawn, leaving the Christians with no accuser but themselves. Dumbfounded, before dismissing the case, the judge cries out like the Roman proconsul Antoninus, 'Unhappy men!' he exclaims, 'Unhappy men! If you are so weary of your lives, is it so difficult for you to find ropes and precipices?'

So speak the comfortable pastor/priests to contemporary Christians, for how could their spiritless lives possibly understand joy in the midst of suffering? Only those whose existence had become so distraught, so shaken that they faced only Him for finding help in securing a happier life. Only they could avoid the suicide or madness that inches forward like the Arctic darkness. These leaders know so little happiness because they experience so little real possiblity.

But the Christian is happier because he lives that possibility among the suffering, of which he himself is one.

Is it not the case, my reader, that what I assert is true, that it is Biblically correct and right?

Does Christianity not teach this by its own example, by the example of the New Testament and that of the original church? Do this and you will see: Move with others into places of desperation and want and you will suffer. Your suffering will be born because your burden will be light.

There are analogies of a lightheartedness amid heavy burdens.

Among the Christians who were brought before the tribunal of the emperor . . . two persons are said to have appeared. . . These were the grandsons of St. Jude the apostle, who himself was the brother of Jesus Christ. Their natural pretensions to the throne of David might perhaps attract the respect of the people and excite the jealousy of the governor; but the meanness of their garb and the simplicity of their answers soon convinced him they were neither desirous nor capable of disturbing the peace of the Roman Empire. They frankly confessed their royal origin and their near relation to the Messiah; but they disclaimed any temporal views, and professed that his kingdom, which they devoutly expected, was of a purely spiritual and angelic nature. When they were examined concerning their fortune and occupation, they showed their hands, hardened with daily labor, and declared they derived their whole subsistence from the cultivation of a farm . . . the grandsons of St. Jude were dismissed with compassion and contempt (p. 289 MLE).

My time in India has been marked by heavy summer

monsoons and flooding. As I walked over a bridge once when the water was high, I watched as a Bihari man, thin, yet powerful enough, hoist his child above the strong current. He was not bent as when he carries fodder on his back.

For him what mattered was keeping his balance, moving forward and reaching the bank. The weight was to me as if he had wings. One thing was needful, to bring his daughter safely to the other side. When he reached dry ground, he did not collapse. He gently set her down to check if she was fine. He said nothing to anyone but looked back over the distance he had come. Congratulate him on his efforts and he will shrug his shoulders, perhaps even feel insulted. There can be no other explanation: he felt no weight. How is it that this man, weakened by little food and so much mud, is able to perform this feat of strength? May we say that this man's love for his child made it as though a weight had been lifted from his back rather than placed upon it? Is it not possible that he would have been swept off his feet had he been alone? Did he not take such joy in his task that the weight transformed the effort into the effortless?

In such a way do Christians take James' command to be joyful amid sufferings. As God promises repeatedly, it is not as hard as all that if we remember we have a reason to carry on, and what lies at the end.

Another example: When I left my room in the Christian quarter of old Jerusalem, I was in a foul mood. Not only was I headed for a year in a West Bank city honeycombed with Hamas, but I had not slept well, had a mammoth of a backpack and was facing a three hour-it should have been forty five minutes but for

Israeli checkpoints-taxi-bus-walk to Nablus, to say nothing of the standing, waiting, fiddling with my passport, transport switches and repetitive questions. All of this in ninety degree heat. Once in Nablus I counted on Arabic hospitality to take it from there.

My facial expressions accurately reflected my thoughts until I sat down in the taxi. Despite my accusative look an old man introduced himself and began to tell me of the British he knew when they controlled the land. There was just about one thing I could do on that trip and that was listen, and his stories were a precursor of what turned out to be an English speaking constellation of storytellers all the way to Nablus. By the time I had arrived I felt built up by trust as well as the blessed wonder of a burden made light.

Ask the Christians. They know. They will tell you that when they first began heeding the hard sayings of Jesus there was no skip in their step, no lightness of being, no feeling of greatness nor thunderous music. They just believed the promises which had brought them out of the hypnosis of the trivial and lifted the sadness that comes with leaving behind all the treasures of Egypt.

Do not expect conformed church authorities to genuinely latch on to Christianity's offer of being happier, which they have never experienced, mistaken a superficial happiness for, or have but have now forgotten it. No, these orthodox entreprenours, who in a Sufi-like trance snub prophetic warnings, including Jesus', continually look for the rapture. This allows them to escape from the world, a world they do not like caring for anyway, as shown by their cars, homes, edifices, and indolent wishdreams.

This has consequences for you, Christian. The rage collected by the gander and geese from all those years of living an unreal life will explode at those who expose it, and you must return a certain gentleness to their anger. You have, in humility, quoted a short verse, or by your simple action made it known that Christianity was your faith, and it is your tactful firmness that forces them to take their rage home and reflect on it. This is the meaning of Christianity's words to not resist evil. Their verbal assaults against you must not be met with the same. It is simply madness to return insult for insult (which is politics), yet patient firmness marks the Christian every time. Not an easy-going lunacy, but a serious-yet-merry gentle courage.

It was said of a church father that his gentleness was such a power that even the pagans respected him. It is a sure sign of Christian contentment, these choices for a happier life, and it must be seized upon now; it is at hand and it is now. For every second you wait upon the good is cause for fear because you have infinitely much more to lose. In the seconds you count on one hand go beyond the immediate, utter one word against your surroundings, gaze one moment longer at the forsaken; in the flash of a sparrow's turn you now hold so much more of Christianity, or perhaps a little more of it; only an instant and that flash will be to you as a dream where you met yourself in iron strength by the Truth. Though your shoulders are stooped and your knees weakened, you are stronger because you remember the moment. Such day-to-day tedium as you know is snapped and you are outside the circle, no longer sunk in the consistency of sin, and you remember.

Uplifted, the gluttonous, trivial, mindlessness of suburban Christendom was vanquished in the moment. 'You have the memory and the Word,' it is Christ who speaks, 'we shall look at what you have done with them when we meet face-to-face in the infinite.'

A Successful Operation: That Christianity has been Removed from the Land

The meekness and resignation which had distinguished the primitive disciples of the gospel was the object of the applause, rather than the imitation, of their successors. The Christians, who now possessed above forty years the civil and ecclesiastical government of the empire, had contracted the insolent vices of prosperity . . . As soon as the enmity of Julian deprived the clergy of the privileges which had been conferred by the favor of Constantine, they complained of the most cruel oppression; and the free toleration of idolaters and heretics was a subject of grief and scandal to the orthodox (p.452 MLE).

What America's pastor/priests have done is to eliminate true evangelism, conversion, and discipleship from the body, as if it were a cancer. For the plain and simple fact is that Christianity exists only in an individual, a couple, a family here and there, and almost never in an organized church; only where there is simplicity, smallness, and prophetic resistance is there a New Testament church.

No question that the conformed leadership, however ridiculous it may sound, has succeeded in nearly drowning

Christianity (with their thirteen hundred megachurches, and countless middle class parishes and churches) by erasing Biblical definitions and converting people to shallow admiration, good intentions, a thought life, and because of their teachers, sheer tokenism.

It would be much simpler if each congregation just hired a well-spoken atheist to denounce Christianity from the pulpit then tie his compensation to the number of converts he obtains.

Clearly he would be well-motivated and if he succeeded in making many converts then it could be said that an effort was made at destroying Christianity.

However unlovely this notion would be to the congregations, it does have the appeal of honesty (for a frontal attack, an honest attack against Christianity is much easier to defend against) and is preferable to what we now have, tens of thousands of tiresome blowhards with the same monetary motive as our salaried atheist in increasing the size of their congregations, which they do by:

(a) getting people to believe they are true Christians and that America is a Christian nation; and

(b) preaching Christianity to a standstill, so that following the Teacher does not matter at all but believing a doctrine about Him does, and letting it go at that.

If one must pay the pastor/priests, then pay them as building supervisors, or foremen, or for being consultants to the construction companies etc., but do not call them shepherds of the flock, and do not call the building a church. If the pastor were to honestly admit before his congregation that he had been making a pretty fair living off the suffering and death of Another and others, and before God he had better start retracing his steps, beginning with giving up his salary, then there is hope for him, he may yet become a Christian pastor.

Before I am accused of not supporting Christian teachers, of muzzling the ox, I can ask where is the Christian teacher, where is the ox that plows? If one is found, give him something to live on.

Yet (this is exactly what the apostle Paul feared and why he accepted no salary), because there has been such abuse-beyond the dreams of mere avarice-of pastoral benefits side jobs (tent-making) have to be a requirement for a Christian minister so as to better judge his Biblical legitimacy.

That is one criteria, but I know all to well that this well-heeled assemblage of mediocrity will not give up their salaries without a fight, and why I believe the congregations should do it for them and ease their pain. Will the congregations follow through and axe their pastor/priest's salaries? Probably not, which is also why becoming a Christian in America has been made nearly impossible, the pastors having so filled the people's minds with nonsense that the offering is automatic.

The result? The pastor cashes his check on Monday for making a fool of God and the people on Sunday, all done in the name of spreading the good news. A salary based upon the number of congregants. Create a scenario where Christianity would have a harder time making inroads.

The apostles discharge their heaviest artillery (they will gather around them a great number of teachers to say what their itching ears want to hear; those who want to make a good impression to avoid being persecuted for the cross; unlike others we do not peddle the word of God for profit; corruption is thinking godliness is a means of financial gain) at what they recognize as the most cunning threat to Christianity, coaxing people into thinking they are Christians while living contrary to Christianity. Congratulations are in order to a leadership that manages, with the text itself sitting on everyone's shelf, to get people to act adversely to what is staring them in the face, to be selective in their readings and application, to turn Christ into a milksop, to make Christianity just a matter of the heart, etc. To withold the truth from people while calling them Christians, this is a job description more criminal than a serial killer's, robbing people of eternity. Even Judas, who chose the less cowardly way of a direct attack, did not take this path.

Let it be shouted throughout the land then that many well-intentioned people, like the god whose pride made him stupid, are being made silly by the pastor/priests. What could be more meaningful now for a person of faith to commit to seriousness? The peeling off of scales, the opening of eyes, the retelling of The Story from a new place to stand, how could this not help but inspire?

Should unbelievers themselves take heart that evangelicalism is finally owning up to its denial, then all the better. A sweeping all-consuming sincerity that engulfs both evangelicals and unbelievers would make jubilant the heavens. Now, finally, reality is being dealt with, and that is the prerequisite to Christian conversion. Unbelievers can at last choose between true religion and unbelief, rather than a parody (which they are right to mock) and unbelief.

What will hinder a true accounting and an authentic assessment of just who is a Christian and who is not? The pastor/priests, for they will step forward immediately to offer their church membership rolls as proof of their effectiveness for Christianity. Who has received Jesus into their heart, taken communion, been baptized, confirmed, responded to the altar call etc. This is suppose to be the criteria that defines the Christian faith of an individual and a nation. An older criteria suggests otherwise:

[The Christians became] the object of universal as well as invidious observation . . . and every member [of the church was] engaged to watch with the most vigilant attention over his own behavior and over that of his brethren, since, as he must expect to incur a part of the common disgrace, he may hope to enjoy a share of the common reputation (p. 256-57 MLE) (italics mine).

The nation has eighty million evangelicals on its church registers, so there has to be that many Christians, or so goes the pastor/priest's thinking. He then sees his task as making these eighty millions better Christians, to oppose abortion, homosexuality, evolution, sexual promiscuity, marital infidelity, contraception (the priests and certain evangelical pastors), and to fight for financial responsibility and civility. That is about the sum of it. If one calls that Christianity, then it is only an approximation, and it should be confessed as such, as lacking in eternity. But if the pastor succeeds in persuading people to call themselves Christians, then eternal regret await that pastor and people who take Christianity so light-mindedly.

It is certainly true to-in certain contexts and parts of the world-call oneself a Christian, or to say one is learning to become one. That the New Testament has no qualms with. Its just this obnoxious trap, this status quo, this unquestioning acceptance of millions of Christians in a Christian land that has to go. If the pastoral leadership wishes that to happen then hundreds of job placement agencies would be pleased to accommodate them in their new lives among the working class poor. If not then may the congregations be that little child that leads them, packing down and moving among the poor without their pastor/priest. If he refuses still, then leave him to an empty building or perhaps even fuller one, for God only knows if this unparalleled farce has played itself out.

Why the Use of the Qualifier But
is Heresy in Christianity

The ambiguous situation of Theophilus [archbishop of Alexandria], a saint, as the friend of Jerome; a devil, as the enemy of Chrysostom; produce a fort of impartiality: yet, upon the whole, the balance is justly inclined against him . . . Eunapius . . . quotes an epistle of Isidore of Pelusium, which reproaches [Theophilus] with the idolatrous worship of gold (p. 345-46 Penguin) (italics mine).

. . . Think of a young man in the throes of a nuptial decision, brought on by the appearance of not one but two young ladies: one of decided beauty and purity of heart, the other her superior in beauty, rather more taken by a zest for life, a joie de' vivre. He chooses the latter and is married.

Ten summers pass and this zest has made him a cuckhold, as he himself grows fat and obsessive, ruing his choice of one over the other. Every spare moment is spent spying on and following the other, living a proxy life as the husband of the other, still sane enough to know the other would never leave her husband for him. He sees his own wretchedness.

But not sane enough. Day by day he feeds his blinding

illusion until he wakes up one morning in the mad belief that he is finally married to the other; he is institutionalized. As a patient he is brought before the doctor, who says to him, 'Sir, your enslavement to a lie, as well as years of allowing yourself to be abused, has led to your present condition. Until you recognize the truth for what it is you will not leave this place, for your way of thinking is a mass of confusion.'

The divided heart is the Qualifier But that leads to consequences the New Testament confidently asserts are far harsher than hospitalization. What is more diabolical than to attach a rejoinder, a witty reply to Christ's words? The Yes but is such a milk sop effeminate strategy to water down Christianity that to bring them together is nothing but word salads. A tisket-a-tasket sing the children but evangelical leaders have a more sophisticated version with their Yes but nonsense:

The preachers recommended the practice of the social duties; but they exalted the perfection of monastic virtue, which is painful to the individual and useless to mankind. [The clergy's] charitable exhortations betrayed a secret wish that [they themselves] might be permitted to manage the wealth of the faithful for the benefit of the poor . . . (p. 399 MLE) (italics mine).

This hedging Yes but, so threatening and dark; this compromise, making the blood run hot with fleshly hope, not knowing what deep sorrow it holds for its owner; this grasping mediation, the individual taking leave of his eternal sense to have it in hand.

Now that the attack on their compromise has been made the

pastor/priests will come forward in droves to insist they have made no compromise with darkness: 'You have ruled out grey areas!'

I say the New Testament does not do otherwise. They ask 'Haven't you made into law and works what the texts have not?' I refer them back to the texts, that we are not free to transgress the very words of the Master, that what IS unclear in His teaching we may address once we begin to obey what is clear. Then, like the evasive 'Who is my neighbor' question, they ask 'Why do you burden us with your unrealistic idealism, saying all or none, everything or nothing?' That I would never do, for I know myself only too well. No, only rid yourself of the Yes but and forge ahead immediately with the confession that you are guilty of using it.

To bring forth the absolute-the assignment of every Christian-is not a task that the present age is at all concerned about, particularly when the Yes but is so persuasive. To confront it one must not send in yet another Qualifier of the reformers. What is demanded is the colussus of remorse/ confession/ repentence. Characterize it like the clever police informer who waits patiently for the sting, pretending to be as corrupt as the gang-while remaining above it-until he has all the information he needs to arrest, then he unmasks himself. In America, it is the authority of the Christian that breaks loose on this slew of orthodox fencers, who so adeptly have cleaved their way through the New Testament with the knife of the Yes but that the absolute is like a dramatic rhetorical advice designed to gain attention. Or, it is similar to the electrical buzz in fencing to let the judges know a score has been made. There is no seriousness about it, it is play just like the use of the word absolute is play. Thus when the unveiling of the Christian occurs, when the pastor/priests are at the high point of their play, the Christian unmasks himself in all seriousness, and now matters are in earnest.

Young man, young woman, you whose desire for Christianity has begun with such enthusiasm, whose sincerity is unquestioned, whose purity of heart vanquishes cynicism, above all things shun the suburban pastor/priests. Shun them as if they were highly polished procurers-which they are, selling the gospel for personal prestige-shun them and have no business with them, these masters of the Qualifier, mimicking the serpent's dialogue with Eve: Does the Lord your God really command you to live sparingly? Does he in fact require you not to become a soldier?

Does he indeed demand you live in proximity to the poor and to your church? These are the questions that undermine sincere Christian faith like a sapper. The appeals to the sensual are exactly what the minister wishes you to engage in. For as sure as misery loves company he loves to make disciples, and that is what you will become if you do not run for dear life from their rhetorical tricks. Humbly recall to yourself daily that you are their teacher/preacher by the power of your purity (this purity will be mocked as 'naivete' by the pastors on Monday, after seeing it on Sunday) and in this way you avoid pride and a show of disrespect. Honor them if they cross your path (they live for this) yet avoid any dialogue with them. If it should happen you are forced into it, answer with a Biblical word, or simply withdraw in silence. Your obedience to the demands of Christianity is what matters.

Young proclaimer of the evangel, know what you are up against. The conformed episcopate has a massive array of finite weapons that can be summed up in the Yes but, which in Biblical language means to have other gods before Him. Take one whose life is either given to the pursuit of comfort or is comfort itself, of which there are plenty of suburban evangelicals. The pastor/priest thinks: there is money to be made, honor to be won here. He preaches to them and to you, young proclaimer: You want eternal security? Come to Christ. You will know a comfort that all the gold in the world cannot bring. Only avoid homosexuality, abortion, obscenity, pornography, drug and alcohol abuse, support the family, and then, blessed assurance, Jesus is yours.

Are you suffering? (at which point his followers bow their heads) Let the Comforter in (pause).

You may wish to give thanks for this splendid gift-at this time we take up our tithes and offerings.

Beware also the congregation, young proclaimer. After New Life's Haggard was relieved of his responsibilities, a church spokesman, with the geese firmly behind him, justified his church's existence with these words: The church is not a man (so one man enjoys superstar status). The church is not a building (so they spend ten million on a building). The church is not an ideology (so they support Democrats or Republicans). The church is a family (so then ten thousand are a family). It is nothing but filthy swill to mix the infinite with the finite as they do.

Your Reverence then defensively shakes his head, 'Yes, we do have a building BUT it is only an instrument of faith. Our heart's desire is truly for eternity.' The congregation has this unspoken understanding with his Reverence on this point, a wink and nod agreement, a 10,000-and-His-Reverence-can't-all-be-wrong attitude that claims we can have every material good and everlasting life too. What most do not know is that this is forcing a break with Christianity (life does not consist in the abundance of things; do not lay up for yourselves treasures on earth; you received your good things and now you are in agony; listen you rich people, weep and wail; this temple [or church building] will be thrown down, etc.). The New Testament then gives two choices: To immediately dispense with the bulk of stuff, or confess they have acted heretically then petition Him for strength in moving forward. If one is young and trapped in the illusion, he must confess he has allowed himself to be used, then under the trained eye of a mature Christian, living in proximity, let the character transformation begin. What the conformed pastorate will fight with all their heart, mind, and soul to protect, with a passion that is as if their own child were being assaulted, as if the gates of Hades were at their door, is for . . . business as usual.

Let the compromise continue as is, no confession, no admission (if it's not broken don't fix it), no character actions, nothing. Having such a knowledge, that one's pastoral/priestly life is a compromise, without the confession there is no hope on the last day. To cowardly drone on and on from the pulpit though, whining and whimpering-these are monkey antics.

I only ask for an ounce of human honesty, that even for an old man who has wasted his whole life living and preaching the Yes but, is enough for him to receive leniency, the pardon that rescues from death. The confession I propose I grasp quite easily because I have not spent my entire adult life pursuing a New Testament existence. Consequently I understand suburban congregants quite well, whom I still believe are hungry enough for the eternal so that a quiet hour would do it, would prompt one to transparently before God admit that the Christianity of the American pastor/priests is not Christianity.

································

The Reformers: Neglecting the Weightier Measures of the Law

Give the American church a little praise, it is said, because it has spawned movements of social transformation, along with its evangelism (e.g. the abolitionists). No doubt the more progressive wing of the church will point out the impact of the Quakers on early America, the Great Awakenings, women's suffrage, Vatican II, certain Catholic Orders who have defended Native Americans, Dorothy Day (house churches, shelters, soup kitchens, non-violent activism), King and the civil rights movement, the Berrigan brothers-who burned draft cards as one would idols-not to mention the ongoing efforts of individual Americans in this land or abroad who live Christianly.

A few long time acquaintances and companions make up this remnant and historically it has ever been the case that there are the seven thousand (i.e. the few) who never bowed the knee to Baal.

So what is the problem? Diversion, charades, and a colossal children's game are the problem.

That the overwhelming majority of America's pastor/priests are board game players of consequence, being well-paid for it, too unwilling to get up from the table, walk out the door and do what the Teacher says. How is it they can get away with this? Answer: the clever child's time honored method: to distract attention. To be the artful dodger, this is what is respected among ill-behaved children. Thus it is so among the clergy, who have a Winkin', Blinkin', and Nod understanding amongst each other that they are in competition to win the majority of the crowd by distracting from earnestness in the cleverest way possible, and that is to take on the identity of a progressive, or reformer (conservative or liberal). They search for the most appropriate mask, and when they find one that makes them appear as a courageous Christian reformer, they are glad beyond belief for it guarantees the attention of women and young girls.

Rather than pointing to and living as if the New Testament mattered, or humbly confessing that it has not, the reformers, like Warren-who write with vapid consistency-become boisterous about trivial matters. They pinch, nip, and tuck some elements of suburban life which have little eternal effect. This is how one can stand up in yet another clerical villa and not say the thing that most needs to be said, that in the name of Christianity the edifice must be sold and the money given to the poor, after first having radically simplified one's own life, to set the example. No, better to waste everybody's time with games: Send more money abroad. Volunteer more hours. Plant more trees. A Bible story and prayer at bedtime, an evening a week of family fun and a smaller car to demonstrate creation care. Suffering! Sacrifice! Self denial! We are making an attempt, they claim. Like the child when asked if he had cleaned his room who responds 'Well,

I'm trying.' The parent looks dubiously upon this answer and check to see what it means.

Christ, the Observer, has eternity to follow the assertions of the reformers, to see how many grains of truth they hold. Do they flirt with the Truth? Is there hypocrisy in their self-denial?

Do they trivialize Christian pain? That man knew a little something when he said that men play at tragedy because they do not believe in the reality of the tragedy which is actually being played in the outside world.

Let the evangelical reformers in both parties ask what the reaction of the early Christians was to Marcus Aurelius, whose character has been most favorably compared to Lincoln's:

The virtue of Marcus Aurelius was of a severer and more laborious kind. It was the well-earned harvest of many a learned conference . . . He regretted that Avidius Cassius, who excited a rebellion in Syria, had disappointed him, by a voluntary death, of the pleasure of converting an enemy to a friend . . . War he detested as the disgrace and calamity of human nature; but when the necessity of a just defense called upon him to take up arms, he readily exposed his person to eight winter campaigns (p. 53 MLE).

Perhaps our reformers could do with a little historical reminder of just how the second century church responded to Marcus' virtue:

[The] refusal to serve [in the army under Marcus] was known to be the normal policy of the Christians-as the reproaches of Celsus (177-180 A.D.) testify . . . while a general distrust of ambition and a horror of

contamination by idolatry entered largely into the Christian aversion to military service, the sense of the utter contradiction between the work of imprisoning, torturing, wounding, and killing, on the one hand, and the Master's teaching on the other, constituted an equally fatal and conclusive objection (p. 245 Cadoux) (italics mine).

But our political evangelical, having spent half his life running from Herod to Pilate, finally establishes a reputation for being on the cutting edge of reform. He is a powerful speaker, an orator, a pastor's pastor, persuasive and passionate-O see the tears he sheds from the pulpit for the integrity of church and country. We will return to our busy democratic reformer.

What next? For our more conservative agent of change the congregation's growth and the pledges and offerings have shown beyond a doubt that it is time for a reassessment. There is a need for modernized hymnals. A larger sanctuary must be built, along with a worship center, an administrative annex, playground, more parking, and for those concerned with the direction our nation is taking, two brilliant new complexes, one dedicated to compassion and the other to the family.

He builds-like the orthodox emperor Justinian-his megachurch [St. Sophia's]:

The new Cathedral of St. Sophia was consecrated by the patriarch . . . and in the midst of the solemn festival [Emperor] Justinian exclaimed with devout vanity, 'Glory be to God, who hath thought me worthy to accomplish so great a work; I have vanquished thee O Solomon!' . . . The edifices of Justinian were cemented with the blood and treasures of his people (p. 715-16 MLE). (italics mine).

The day no longer tarries when our reformer steps up to the microphone to address the thousands. The sermon on this day is entitled: Faith is being certain of what we do not see, then he preaches what the congregation calls a dynamic sermon and what was especially meaningful was the story of his trip to give the invocation at the inaugeration of a President, where he felt the unseen presence of the Holy among America's political/ religious leaders.

But, my readers, would Christ have even gone to the Roman Forum after having ridiculed that selfsame leadership? I mean Good Night, the pastor was smack in the middle of all that power that was very much seen. Well, you understand him. The trip, the prayer, the influence wielded- all for the good! How could he pass up an opportunity to witness like that?

The corporate life of the men in suits has the blasphemous affrontery to call itself obedience to God's will. If it is indeed God's will then why not call the revival of the gladiatorial games under Commodus Christian reform? Why not call the benediction bestowed by the chaplain on the pilots of the Enola Gay before they annihilated Japanese cities a new liturgical innovation? Truly anything fits this definition of reform.

Yet suppose our reformer does will that evangelicalism becomes purified, and reproaches himself first as per the command: can he be said to hesitate in bringing forth true Christianity? Yes, and if he still lacks (the distinction between what hesitates for the Truth and a full scale commitment to the Truth is complex and painfully difficult to discern) then this lack cannot be so easily detected, which is more troubling in a sense because the life that is lived is Christianity, far and above what middle class pastors on up do. But it hedges in two ways that are barely noticeable.

When he wishes to force the ethical by politics there is hesitancy.

Where did Bonhoeffer-alas Dietrich, in all your prophetic courage-just once go vitally wrong?

Was it in his attack upon the state church, the wet nurse to Hitler? Was it in his repeated denunciations of the National Socialists as godless? No, and no again. It was in yielding to the last temptation of Christ, to become political, to enjoy a self-assertion he never needed to employ, to call out the defenses and captain Hitler's assassination.

There are serious Christian reformists then who err on the side of self-assertion, of taking the kingdom of God by storm. There was the literal and political embrace of Obama by Jim Wallis (whom one could call the Lactantius of Constantine), then the haughty claims of other prominent reformers to be Democrats. This is hesitation, hedging, and a step back. If true Christianity is to bore into America it will not come by means of church sponsored compassion forums for presidents-this is battling the air. True Christian presence is generally marked by tedious slowness that will frustrate many and turn them away from the Good.

Second, their writings reflect hesitation through their passive approach. The emphasis of Christian men-Campolo, Sider, Foster, Wills, and Wallis-has been largely Socratic, that what is needed is to overcome ignorance with better theology, then just show the evangelical the Good and he will do it. The New Testament is there too-in the background. This is an effeminate reversal of priority. Like the artist who details the shapely nose, at the price of the eye that pierces, the Demand is not foremost for fear of offending the evangelical crowd too much (they offend to a degree), whose patronage puts meat on the table for their publishers. Is this hesitation? Even if his life is just and full of faith, even if his writings express Christianity, even if his soul cries out in confession (for that is Christianly correct), particularly if he has shown himself to be a serious Christian: could he be hesitating? No, apparently not, but he is.

The politicization of Christians as democrats manifests ill temper and is like the child who sits down in the grocery store and refuses to budge until he gets what he wants. Their decision to bring politics to bear upon the evangel shows they do not grasp that God acts slowly to give people time to repent themselves, of their own free will, to freely determine if they will serve Him. They refuse to acknowledge the Biblical maxim that Christ is doing just fine without politics. Recall that the faithful servants, the heroes of the Book of Hebrews, judged by their contemporaries, accomplished nothing.

Bonhoeffer would have us learn from his one and only wrong move. Take up the Good, he would say, and put on your walking shoes in keeping with the humility of the unprofitable servant. Act for the Good, not permitting your left hand knowledge of what your right hand is doing-which is politics-as a true striver moves past the political victory to the eternal triumph.

As for our more artful dodgers-the Warrens, Perkins, Jakes

and Hunters-one might think after hearing just one parable from the New Testament these nincompoops would head straight for their homes, go to their rooms, shut the doors, beat their breasts black and blue, then act immediately toward character transformation. No racking of brains is required, if there is a brain left to rack.

I do not think it is too much to ask that they cease their criminal abortion of Christianity and change their ways. Their notion of reform has become just so sadly comical that it recalls the tale of the bishop of yesteryear who, to bless the masses, stationed himself on a pedestal alongside a road and clunked people on the head with a wooden cross as they walked by, prompting one wry bystander to ask if the bishop had a wooden head as well.

Thou Shalts for this Present Age

I am inclined to suspect that a large majority of the prelates sacrificed their secret conscience to the temptations of hope and fear . . . the Christians had wandered far away from the simplicity of the gospel: nor was it easy for them to discern the clue and tread back the mazes of the labyrinth (p. 873 MLE).

The church must be ready, like the apostle John, to be pulled along to places it does not wish to go; and this is not a figure of speech.

It must be a reigning truth that each church body is composed of no more than fifty to seventy people, not just because this was the maximum number of followers Christ had, but the numbers of the house fellowships of the early church. This will be a crucial criteria of whether that church will be a Biblical church or not. Further, in neighborhoods of real deprivation they practice Christianity, charitable to the point of pain. There, some will be trained to be sent to where Christianity has not been heard, or lands where their lives are at considerable risk.

Bishops, pastors, elders, and deacons are elected based upon evidence, the evidence of servant leadership, and not because they talk the most, or tell you they are gifted pastorally or prophetically, that they had a divine revelation, vision, dream, but that it is clear in their character. There is a little something of the Pauline list of sufferings in their history that marks them as one to emulate. They have demonstrated self-denial, and deny themselves in ways that the fellowship is able to see daily.

Be of sober mind O reader when it comes to this matter of numbers, for the true pastor will attack the false gospel of quantity over quality by striving to imitate the early church (and its companion in poor nations) with their small and local congregations. To recall that they (the small fellowships in downtrodden places) are this way because of poverty, persecutions, and the demands inherent to Christianity-this is to be Christianly sober-minded:

According to the irreproachable testimony of Origen, the proportion of the faithful was very inconsiderable when compared with the multitude of an unbelieving world . . . (p. 271 MLE).

Let the battalions of well-fed pastor/priests have their way in front of the mirror, if that is what they covet. It is inconceivable for me to think of this happening in the places where I have lived and seen Christianity as a way of life; there are simply too many obstacles there that hinder Christians from falling in love with themselves or their group, so much straightforward disgust directed toward them that they are either thrust into New Testament living or outside the church.

If the Christian seeks to be found in faith on earth-what else is it to express Christ in America?

After the confession that you have allowed yourself to be misled, so abominably misled that if not for your own version of Balaam's sharp donkey you were heading straight for perdition-this is an honesty that compels action-you will be led to a small remnant within your church who have made the same confession. What is secret now becomes public. Your authentic church is being established. The elected pastor among your little flock will determine, after pursuing New Testament criteria for crucial decision-making, the poor neighborhood where you live in immediate proximity to one another.

Would you doubt the demand to live within walking distance of your brothers and sisters of faith? Why is it that now, solitary Christians, who sincerely strive to will Christ's will, are so spread out, so scattered that they see each other at best twice a week? Why abandon oneself in this way? Why should individualism make practicing Christianity so hard? Near one another the sojourn of prophetic and pastoral ministry begins.

Among you there will be a husband or a wife whose spouse is unwilling to go there, in the situation of being a Joanna, whose husband Chuza was Herod's steward. She finds a way. So it must go with the wife or husband who, chained to a suburban neighborhood, sets out to be a part of the genuine church, being the example Peter wrote of.

From the point of confession there is a very careful examination of one's vocation, to determine if it meets the Deuteronomic standard of choosing a life that is meaningful and ethical. A martial or armaments manufacturing career is outlawed in a New Testament church. No Christian carries a deadly weapon. Any high juridical position is forbidden, as it was in the early church and for the same reasons. Earthly stewardship is a key criteria; if there is ethical confusion let the pastor-whose authority is based on daily sacrifice-decide.

When the conformed clergy hear this they will have the nerve to act surprised, and claim it is not they who have become too powerful, but those who demand they repent themselves of power. What must emerge is a similar historical reaction to Roman clerical power:

Under the successors of Constantine, in the peace and luxury of the triumphant church the . . . bishops . . . were now opposed by the murmers of many simple or rational Christians, who appealed to the evidence of the texts, of facts, and of the primitive times, and secretly desired the reformation of the church (870, 872 MLE).

Christians now, as then, walk into large cathedrals, mega-churches, new edifices of every type, kind, and denomination-all dedicated to the propagation of the gospel-astonished at how such a such a thing could be called a church. Recognizing that what they hear from the pulpit is doctrinally correct, they are ready to burst at what they see surrounding that doctrine. Mature contemporary Christians must stand outside these spacious wastes of time and money and cry out in truly evangelic sermons. This, with the knowledge they will be hated, ignored, or opposed by the departing masses. These same masses will, just as in the New Testament, believe that by their opposition they are rendering service to God. A friend once walked up to the platform during the service, folded up an American flag next to the pulpit, and placed it on the altar. This is true Christian liberty, something that official Christian leadership has alienated itself from.

Luxury-compared to the developing world-is what killed Christianity and only the gospel preached among the poor can bring it back:

The charity of Deogratias, bishop of Carthage . . . generously sold the gold and silver plate of the church to purchase the freedom of some, to alleviate the slavery of others, and to assist the wants and infirmities of a captive multitude whose health was impaired by the hardships which they had suffered in their passage from Italy to Africa. By his order, two spacious churches were converted into hospitals; the sick were distributed into convenient beds, and liberally supplied with food and medicines; and the aged prelate repeated his visits both in the day and night, with an assiduity that surpassed his strength and a tender sympathy which enhanced the value of his services (p. 624 MLF).

When Christianity refers to the poor it is speaking of economics, of course, but also of lonely, abandoned, and special needs children, of the mentally ill, refugees, prisoners, the elderly forsaken by a technological society, those hounded by immigration, the incapacitated and the dying, and single mothers frought with concern, of women savaged. The good news is first meant for them:

. . . the body of the people [generally] is condemned to obscurity, ignorance, and poverty. The Christian religion, which addressed itself to the whole human race, must consequently collect a far greater number

*of proselytes from the lower than from the superior ranks of life . . .
Our serious thoughts will suggest to us that the apostles themselves
were chosen by Providence among the fishermen of Galilee, and that
the lower we depress the temporal condition of the first Christians,
the more reason we shall find to admire their merit and success. It is
incumbant on us diligently to remember that the Kingdom of Heaven
was promised to the poor in spirit, and that minds afflicted by calamity
and the contempt of mankind cheerfully listen to the divine promise of
future happiness; while on the contrary, the fortunate are satisfied with
the possession of this world; (p. 272 MLE) (italics mine).*

What is unclear about Christ's command, that the gospel
is first preached to the poor? What is it that Dobson, Osteen,
Warren, the Grahams and their followers do not comprehend?
The pastor/ priests/evangelists have ALWAYS suffered a lack of
compassion when they do not live next to or with the poor. Far
from: mammon, prestige, perfect fitness, and so forth-in no way
is this related to Christianity.

The New Testament answer to the question How then shall
we live is to hold to the laws of love.

To rebuke oppressive officials, provide options for work
other than soldiering, allow the mother with child to see her
way out of infanticide, to persuade prostitutes and procurers;
infidelity, addictions, the evils of predatory lending, slumlords
and medical costs that trade physical health for debtors suicide-
nothing escapes the concerned eye of the prophetic church.

A connection must be made with a church in a poor nation so
that both churches may strive to live simply and at approximately

the same level economically as per the command-one spirit, body, Lord. The sacrifice of striving to live like your counterpart, in, say, Sudan, is a requirement (Paul: Our desire is that there may be equality) of practical concern as well, for in America the flabby outnumber porn addicts and swindlers. One look around you in the megachurch and you would think the flabby, not the poor in spirit, will inherit the earth.

No matter what works the New Testament churches in America undertake, divine forgiveness applies only-mark this-only when one confesses, confesses that one is a sinner in need of grace.

Luther wrote somewhere that one who commits boundless crimes throughout the course of a lifetime, perpetrated unimaginably malevolent deeds and daily-yet quiets himself to say: God be merciful to me a sinner-that this person has an infinitely greater chance of forgiveness than the one who for the love of the truth bears the cross for seventy years then errs by clinging to the thought that he now deserves an ounce of mercy. Such a spiritual self-murder has all the elements of tragic pathos-like one imprisoned in a dungeon since childhood who at an old age slips his neck into a noose-just before the king's pardon arrives. But this parable does not convey the unspeakable torment of what would happen if one assumes that Eternity owes one something.

Christianity, Mohammed, Church Authority and Thee

The use of fraud and perfidy, of cruelty and injustice, were often subservient to the faith; and Mohammed commanded or approved the assassination of the Jews and idolaters who had escaped from the field of battle. By the repetition of such acts, the character of Mohammed must have been gradually stained; and the influence of such pernicious habits would be poorly compensated by the practice of the personal and social virtues which are necessary to maintain the reputation of a prophet among his sectaries and friends. Of his last years, ambition was the ruling passion; and a politician will suspect that he secretly smiled (the victorious imposter!) at the enthusiasm of his youth and the credulity of his proselytes (p. 930-31 MLE).

In the spirit of Christ's parable of the log in the eye, it must be preached in Christendom that Islam has far more to fear from Christendom than vice versa, for Islam cannot even approach the contemporary scales when it comes to what Christendom has already mastered, the global threats of annihilation by war or warming.

But the most serious competitor to the Judas kiss of American church authority (in the danger it places upon spirit) is Islam. The conformed church fears Islam mightily, and have thus hidden behind the false military curtain of the West. They are vaguely aware of just what Islam is, the horrors it espouses, the propagation of torture, the ongoing practice of slavery, the general treatment of women as property, the constant suspicion of having been insulted, the jihad, the hatred of the infidel despite the sheik's and apologist's claim of universal toleration. The West is correct to know it; and whereas those who confess Christ have no excuse, Islam has its own justification.

But we will get to this later.

Having lived several years in the Middle East, total immersion into Islamic society is a good teacher. I know now better than I knew before that even though Mohammed of Mecca and Jesus of Nazareth both trod the dust of the Middle East, that is absolutely where the similarity ends.

What is so startling though is how religious and social critics could miss this, that the American clergy has so actively imitated Mohammed, however inadvertently. One could say this imitation is invisible, similar to racism in America being so prevalent that it too is invisible. This is exactly how it is with Islam's influence on our own court flatterers.

Two examples come to mind of which the entire conformed church has become guilty. When the American soldier is commissioned by the church, takes his Bible to the battlefront, invokes Christ's protection in a prayer group before going out on patrol, it is an exact equivalent to what the Crusaders did, and the Crusade was a zealous desire to surpass the jihad. The Crusade included a guarantee of salvation, and now when the evangelical soldier dies in battle (O abuse of youth!), his home church treats it in the same way:

If they fell, the spirit of the Latin clergy did not hesitate to adorn the tomb with the crown of martyrdom; and should they survive, they could expect without impatience the delay and increase of their heavenly reward. They offered their blood to the Son of God, who had laid down his life for their salvation: they took up the cross, and entered with confidence into the way of the Lord. His providence would watch over their safety; perhaps his visible and miraculous power would smooth the difficulties of their holy enterprise (p. 1054 MLE).

This has historical correspondence to the present day, especially if the American soldier is an evangelical. But it was Muhammed who provided the blueprint:

. . . The martial apostle [Mohammed] fought in person at nine battles or seiges; and fifty enterprises of war were achieved in ten years by himself or his lieutenants. The Arab continued to unite the professions of a merchant and a robber; and his petty excursions for the defense or the attack of a caravan insensibly prepared his troops for the conquest of Arabia . . . 'The sword,' says Muhammed, 'is the key of heaven and hell; a drop of blood-shed in the cause of God, a night spent in arms, is of more avail than two months of fasting or prayer: whosoever falls in battle, his sins are forgiven: at the day of judgment his wounds shall be resplendent as vermilion and odiferous as musk; and the loss of his limbs shall be supplied by the wings of angels and cherubim' (p. 919-20 MLE) (italics mine).

The Roman emperors had already been moving in this direction, but with Mohammed Christendom now had a serious adversary and had to outdo him with the Crusade. With Mohammed's arrival the definition of holy war is expanded, for now if a religious leader chooses to go to war without religious sanction, he can do it for some other reason, and indeed he must if there is just cause. So the Just War is given an even greater impetus, that as long as a certain criteria are met then a President must go to war whether it be preemptive, preventive, defensive etc. The important thing to remember is evangelical authorities have copied Mohammed perfectly in that if a religious/political leader just thinks-with the help of Just War preachers like the Grahams-there is a threat, he and his people must take the bloody path, and that this is Christianity.

A second example of conformed church leaders seeking to be religious/political powers like Mohammed: Whenever one hears Biblical verses being flung back and forth in political campaigns or from the press room in the White House (Without a vision the people perish; Fight the good fight; You are either for us or against us etc.) be certain that Mohammed is there, Mohammed is whispering in their ears. What he did was to lay the groundwork for the absolute unity of church and state:

From the Atlantic to the Ganges, the Koran is acknowledged as the fundamental code not only of theology but of civil and criminal jurisprudence; and the laws which regulate the actions and the property of mankind are guarded by the infallible and immutable sanction of the will of God (p. 942 MLE).

Hence political leadership is also religious leadership, a situation in which Robertson and Dobson would rejoice, because then the separation between church and state would be eliminated.

They would not dare to label it a theocracy, or attempt to undermine the constitution (this would frighten the educated), but would incrementally erode that separation. The Bush and Trump victories were as if fairies danced in their dreams for evangelical leaders, having come under the historical influence of Mohammed and having sought the approval of men and politics. So a President is chosen because he quotes the Bible and evangelicals honor him for his Christianity etc. The political head is now the de facto religious head, and it does not matter if you call it a theocracy or not. He is God's ambassador on earth. His military initiatives and political decisions come from the Holy Spirit-so the thinking goes.

A constitutional separation of church and state is anathema to the Koran, the serious Muslim and Mohammed. Most Muslims cannot even conceptualize a true democracy, which is why dialogue on this matter is almost fruitless; just how many times can one hear that this is unIslamic and so is that and on and on. You hear this even in Muslim partial democracies, which are rare enough.

It was just after Yassir Arafat was elected president in the Palestinian territories that I began work at a university in Nablus. In an enthusiastic discussion class with students whom I otherwise liked, I made the ridiculous mistake of asking each class member to voice their dream for the world. Fully three quarters of the class described the same thing, the establishment of a Muslim caliphate on earth.

This is what they were calling for: Now let the reader keep in mind that Mohammed was not unaware of notions of toleration, the free exchange of ideas, foreigner's rights etc. He had at his disposal at least Biblical oral tradition, as well as some Christians in Mecca and Medina who had not taken up the sort of Christianity prevailing at the time-worship of relics, images, martyrs, saints and angels. There were also active Jewish communities in Mecca, his early home, and numerous chances to engage both groups, which he most certainly did. Any future caliphate would no doubt reflect his own treatment of Christians during his reign, which was ambiguous, which accounts for the unequal treatment they receive under Islamic governments.

A pernicious tenet has been imputed to the Mohammedans, the duty of extirpating all other religions by the sword. This charge of ignorance and bigotry is refuted by the Koran, by the history of the Moslem conquerors, and by their legal and public toleration of the Christian worship. But it cannot be denied that the Oriental churches are depressed under their iron yoke; that in peace and war they assert a divine and indefeasible claim of universal empire; and that in their orthodox creed the unbelieving nations are continually threatened with the loss of religion or liberty (p. 1051 MLE).

Mohammed was very much aware of the martial strength of the Latins and the Greeks, thus this shrewd general and politician took that into account in his confusing and ambiguous edicts. He also knew them to be the enemy of his real enemy, the Jews, who had treated his visions and doctrine with such contempt. He had desired the Jews view him as their last and final prophet, but they obstinately refused and thus his sentence on the Jewish tribes: The Kainoka were driven out of their homes in Syria. The Nadhirites were exiled. The Koraidha were chained and led into the town center, some seven hundred, then marched into a mass grave where Mohammed approved the ensuing massacre. He moves on to the city of Chaibar, seen as a beacon of Jewish power in Arabia, forces it into submission then tortures the tribe's chief to learn where its treasure is.

Whereas true Christianity is the most tolerant religion in the world-except when it comes to nonviolent, noncooperation with any misrepresentations of itself-what Mohammed does to those 'not of the Book' anticipates even more what a caliphate would look like, such as female captives in war being given to jihadis as wives and concubines, then he generously declares that in their sale mothers should not be separated from their children.

All this, of course, a result of war upon the infidel, the unbeliever. With Mohammed war came naturally. Contempt for the unbeliever is virtually on every other page of the Koran. It is a part of his teaching, commandment, that the whole world will become Muslim through Arabic victories. When a veiled student told me that now was America's time but some day it will be Islam's, and for that reason she felt sorry for me, I knew exactly what she was talking about. By then I had familiarized myself with what happened immediately after Mohammed's death. Taking the cue from their leader, savage attacks began in every direction except the heavily garrisoned north. A century later that too falls with the conquest of Spain and North Africa, then India to the east. For the inhabitants it was as if lightening had struck, a blitzkrieg Attila could appreciate.

Compare their conversions by war to the conversions by sanctity of the early church, whose members resisted the sword for three hundred years and even then large numbers still rejected its use, seeing it for what it was, a diabolical appeasement. Its acceptance opened the church up to divorce, no longer being the bride of Christ. But from the very beginning Mohammed kisses the blade and calls it the means to paradise. All this with him having in easy reach Christian oral history, if not a New Testament.

Islam's claim on Jerusalem comes out of a tale in the Koran. Mohammed is flown (neither a vision nor allegory) by a horselike animal, called a Borak, from Mecca to Jerusalem. There he and the angel Gabriel leave for the heavens where they are hailed by angels, prophets and Old Testament figures, each from their own mansion. He travels alone now and passes through a veil near to the throne of Allah, who touches his shoulder to warm the chill in his heart. When finished he returns to Jerusalem then back to Mecca.

With regard to his private life his present day followers are quick to defend his actions on the basis of cultural context, that he was only doing what any seventh century man did. This is used to justify acting on desires he outlaws in others. He appropriates the wife of his adopted son Zeid, then acquires a wife (I use the term with disgust) by marrying the nine year old daughter of Abubakar, who establishes the caliphate.

The excuse of cultural context is the first thing that springs from the lips of educated Muslims in debate. But for the uneducated majority its a non-issue because Mohammed can do what he likes. In fact, you risk death in many places for even bringing up the topic. The cultural context excuse can be examined by looking at the first forty years of his life.

Two brief trips to Syria as a boy with his uncle would not have given him much in the way of life options, particularly since he had no knowledge of Syriac. However, pilgrims came to Mecca from everywhere to worship idols or do business. Naturally he listened to the belief and observed the practice of the Jews and Christians. The Syrian monk would have crossed his path as well as the Persian academic, each knowing Mohammed's native tongue. But this was not enough; we learn from his adolescence that solitude would be his goal. Thus he withdrew every year for a month to the cave of Hera, an hour's walk from Mecca, to meditate upon religion. So it was until the age of forty, when he emerged with a mixture of Judeo-Christian theology and visions, proclaiming there is only one God, and later that he himself was God's final messenger.

The virtues of which Muslims perpetually praise him recall certain practices of the monks. He is hailed for precepts of prayer, fasting and alms, all of which are inscribed as Koranic law but the latter receives the most attention because of its outward generosity. The tithe of a tenth of one's income is mandated and if one has a guilty conscience, the tenth becomes a fifth in making reparations to the offended party. It is argued that his concern for the poor grew out of his own experience, which makes him so appealing as a prophet, because of his identification with the common man. And not just that. His sins and attributes, along with his ability to unite Arabs around 'a Book,' make him out to be the messenger of God, and this is passionately believed by all Muslims. He swept the floor, mended his own clothes and made no mention of a soldierly diet of dates, barley bread and water. He took no wine but on holy days set up feasts for his entourage.

His more tolerant and merciful leanings relate precisely to his personal history, as do his commands to war against the unbeliever. His conversion to more peaceful writings was an obvious result of fear for his own life, since he was living in Mecca where the citizens had taken deep offense at his life and words. When he travels to Medina, his sanctuary, the Koran takes a dramatic turn toward vengeance and forced conversion. His patience with Mecca was gone, oral argument was exhausted and the force documented in the eighth and ninth chapters of the Koran is put into play.

Islamic scholars point to his success as proof of his authenticity. Many Muslims are raised with solely Koran in hand, knowing only his success, and thus have more excuse. But those with even a slight knowledge of history know that the millenia are full of successful warlords who have wooed the mob by their ability to turn a phrase and lead an army. What does it prove that yet another commoner should overthrow a political or religious powerbase and replace it with his own?

There have been rebels who came from greater depths than Mohammed, overcome more and conquered more. Here was just another fanatic who stumbled upon the formula for success through contemplation. That formula being the reasonable, historical and comforting notion of one God (Christianity is more trinitarian than monotheistic and this must be stressed), uniting this with certain carnal pleasures such as many wives, spoils and victory, pleasures that are magnified in the afterlife.

Some Muslims know this but most are unsuspecting, with no desire to become suspicious. In this they resemble Christendom in relation to New Testament Christianity, but evangelicals will be held to far greater account, for to whom much is given . . .

But the hair-trigger to take offence, the snap judgment that one (or Islam) is insulted, the hunger to offer oneself and one's sons up to blood revenge, an entire nation's fatwa, all this belongs to Mohammed, whereas there is none of this in Christ or the early church.

. . . [Mohammed was] commanded to propogate his religion by the sword, to destroy the monuments of idolatry, and without regarding the sanctity of days or months, to pursue the unbelieving nations of the earth . . . But the mild tenor of the evangelic style may explain an ambiguous text that Jesus did not bring peace on earth but a sword: his patient and humble virtues should not be confounded with the intolerant zeal of princes and bishops who have disgraced the name of the disciples (p. 918 MLE) (italics mine).

I was more or less aware of this when I took the teaching post at what some called Hamas U in Nablus. Mid-year I instigated an official debate I knew I could not outwardly win. The reason was simple: If I displayed my knowledge and challenged the character of Mohammed, then half the students in a packed hall would have risen up. I had already been threatened and could tell from the nervous glances from friends and colleagues they were hoping I would not be so mad as to attack their prophet.

Not prepared to die yet, and in this manner, I thought just making a statement for Christianity would encourage the few Christians in the crowd and perhaps prompt some reflection from the Muslims listening intently. My approach then was to defend the trinity by rational argument-I saw the near futility of this-and lash out as hard as I could at American church leadership as unChristian and no example for anybody. To present the Truth there, three miles from Jacob's Well, this was my purpose. Here was no debate conducted under Robert's Rules of Order; nothing like those debates at Cambridge between Muslim and Christian that come under the protection of civilized academic protocol. True I was thinking of my own life, but also those of the minority Christians in the city. The sheik (a religious teacher) who spoke for Islam was an affable enough fellow whom I had met before-he too looked nervous on my behalf-and just as I thought he immediately accused the actions of Christendom in the West, commenting on the fabulous Islamic civilization of the twelfth century. Then he made the inevitable witticism about the trinity (a concept that strikes Muslims as amusing and polytheist) which drew a laugh. We went back and forth for an hour and I had to listen to the sarcasm and ridiculous justifications of Islam, like the reason women are treated as they are is due to men who hold them in such high regard they must be protected etc. At the end we shook hands and returned to our respective classes. I knew my witness had been limited, no blood-witness this day, but with Governance's aid a witness nevertheless.

I cannot overstate enough here that inspite of Islam, I have encountered astonishing warmth and lifelong friendships in every Arabic neighborhood I have ever lived in. Hospitality that has endured thousands of years cannot be so easily erased by a hostile imposter in a mere fourteen hundred years. This fact became clear every time I sat down with the historically ferocious Bedouins who used to camp near my village in Egypt. Though we had to work hard at comprehending the slightest matter, we could still sit in the silent generosity of his tent. I recalled the reception given the toddler Jesus there, and Moses before that. In fact, most Egyptians are more Egyptian than they are Muslim, though for their very lives they would not admit it. Before a political Israel forced itself through Palestine, the Palestinians were well known for their hospitality to the foreigner; now mistrust has increased exponentially, but not with all. The Palestinians knew my nationality and they also know who pays for the Israeli weaponry that makes their lives so miserable. Yet they were friendly if not always personable. Traditional hospitality explains why very few westerners have ever been taken hostage in Gaza or the West Bank; and when they have been, hostages were treated as guests under the concept of 'forced hospitality.'

The warmth I received from families produced an awkward profit, I think, when from compulsion I told them the reason we were friends was that they ignored the Koran. They took this as a contradictory compliment, and a disagreement arose as to what had the greatest influence on their treatment of the alien, tradition or Islam. They said both. With no other Muslims around, some would tell me they did not care much for religion anyway.

Returning to Mohammed, the New Testament house church in America has to make some crucial choices. Of course their main focus is the re-evangelism of the American church. Of this I have said enough. But there will be some among the optimal number of fifty to seventy (in each church) who will heed the command to go to the nations, to speak of Christianity where He is unknown and be prepared to suffer for doing so. Only the Christianly mature are sent out long term, prepared for the loving confrontation with Islam that is inevitable. To follow the way I have taken, which involves an attack on Mohammed's credibility, one-to-one with a Muslim friend, is playing with fire but profitable in that it wears on the Muslim's conscience over time, and Muslims are faster than the pastor/priests at arriving at the truth of what it means to be a Christian. Another and far more dangerous way, one that speeds up the decision making process considerably (!), is to publicly reproach Mohammed, as did the monks at the Damascus gate in Jerusalem eight hundred years ago. Your life then will almost certainly be forfeit unless you are imprisoned for protection like Paul. It also means the Muslim must make a character versus character choice, the Christian's integrity and reputation against Mohammed's. Punish the Christian and live with a bad conscience or let him go on and violate fully half the commands ever uttered against the infidel by Mohammed.

In my last days in Kafr Manfi, Egypt, I ventured this by telling my sixth grade class, whose life and future I was deeply concerned about, that 'Mohammed was a bad man.' One hot tempered boy raged that he would report me to the principal and did, so she and the department head were laying in wait to point their fingers and warn me against my words. The tension was such that I left the school to get some tea.

I honestly did not know what I was going to return to, a crowd of infuriated villagers-who knew me as their neighbor-or an empty school. There was no one there. The elitest school officials, who never acknowledge the poor villagers, had kept what I had said to themselves because to speak with a lower class Muslim was too far beneath them. So much for the egalitarianism of Islam.

The house church in America will send out more mature Christian ambassadors than any mega or middle class church, any Warren initiative, CBN sponsored, or Billy Graham funded organization could ever conceive of, and better, for the New Testament will mark the sending church while the conformed church leadership remains scared of anything unusual (note how many megachurches have armed security with orders to shoot to kill). The pastor/priest himself sits in his leathered, well decorated office, agitated whenever Mohammed's visage appears in his mind, for this man has infinitely so much more to lose.

O Christian, you who yearn for every people group to hear the Truth, who gazes at pictures of young and old in foreign lands and loses himself day and night in thoughts of being there; how earnestly I urge you to obey the command and leave the conformed church leaders who can do nothing for you except harm you eternally. Find the like-minded among you and gather yourselves for the house church in the neighborhood of diversity and deprivation where you can receive your training, readying you for a people where you become what you were meant to become.

Forget not the Muslim, so abominably deceived by an eloquent fanatic. Forget not the one who ignores Mohammed for the sake of his own beloved tradition, the Arab, who outwardly espouses Islam but in his life welcomes you by his hearth. Know this, man or woman whose spirit is lifted by holy thoughts, that the darkness of Islam awaits thee.

The same hospitality which was practiced by Abraham and celebrated by Homer is still renewed in the camps of the Arabs . . . [they] embrace without enquiry or hesitation the stranger who dares to confide in their honor and to enter their tent. His treatment is kind and respectful: he shares the wealth or the poverty, of his host; and after a needful repose, he is dismissed on his way, with thanks, with blessings, and perhaps with gifts (p. 896 MLE) (italics mine).

An HIV Child's Self-Contemplation

What is the character of silent suffering for the sake of love?

. . . The new sect of Christians was almost entirely composed of the dregs of the populace, of peasants and mechanics, of boys and women, of beggars and slaves . . . (Penguin p. 183).

[The scene is a narrow gully in the Wazirabad slum on the outskirts of New Delhi, nine year old Rupa Kumar is walking away from a group of children standing outside a neighbor's window watching television. Rupa is HIV positive, having contracted the virus at birth from her mother]:

Those children do not know me well, or they would have driven me off as the adults do my mother. Good thing that TV show held their interest or one of them might have recognized me.

Even if they were nice to me, as only my HIV friend Choti is, we could not play long together. I am too weak for more than a short walk now.

Mother said I looked the princess in my purple dress,-found by that elderly widow rummaging through a garbage dump-that my mother washed. I wonder if I would live to be a woman how I would look in a sari . . . Sometimes, when I watch the boys play cricket, I imagine them showing off for me. Right now though, if I stop to watch just for a moment, some cry out and curse me, saying I have bad karma. Well, there are things I know about their parents, especially their fathers. Why is it I must be silent about them? Why can I not spit at the mothers who mock my mother? Was it her fault my father was unfaithful to her with some prostitute along the route of his truck driving job?

I should be in school now, for whatever else I am, I am smarter than the cricket boys.

That TV show about America-so many tourists come from there-showing all those big buildings. They have a religion there the same as our Benny Hinn, where they build temples to what they say is one God. Those temples are so large they cost billions of rupies. The adults laughed at the amount.

I like talking with the god, when I am alone in our plastic shack. I listen to him. He never interrupts me, and occasionally good things happen when I need them to. I remember when we had a clinic near our home and one of the followers of the god of the Americans, Christ is what she called him-he is probably one of our gods too-came to give me this drug cocktail for my HIV, O and did it make me feel better! I did cartwheels for the tourists that day and earned a hundred rupees!

Soon after, Kate, the nurse at the clinic, sat down next to me and told me she had to go for they were closing the clinic. No more rupees to keep it open. No more drug cocktails. She looked upset and spoke with a sharper tongue than usual. I understand why.

Kate said the church's India fund was short because the money was going other places. She acted like she wanted to say more, stopped herself, gave me an embrace, said she would pray to her Christ for me, then left.

Kate has a great love for her god, yet when she stopped talking, I know it was because she thought I was not ready to hear it. She was thinking what I was thinking, that in India rich people spend so much on themselves and their children and do not care at all for outcasts like me, or those with HIV, or the lower castes-again me. Kate was thinking that in America, with their great temples, it is the same way. Different religion, same results.

[She arrives at her shack, sits down cross-legged and makes a fist]

What help are churches and temples to me? Why can't all those followers of Christ be like Kate? Should they not give us the clinic and enough rupees for bread? We work so hard for nothing. And what DO they end up giving us? They give us the great chance to do cartwheels, to beg and scrounge through dumps. They think they are doing their god a service by letting us be so bad off that we learn how to trust god by having nothing. So what we get is a scrap from their opulent tables and the great privilege to look at one of their fabulous white male versions of Hollywood-what they call evangelical pastors-and a pat on our heads to make themselves feel better before their Christ-sure, such mercy! Yet when these pastors and their camera crews are finished here they immediately head back to a multi-star hotel, which also shows how pitiful their efforts are at mercy, how they lie to god and us. Shall I curse them in my solitude?

That I will not do. Better to be in silent grief, to suffer my death quietly than to be one of those women mad with bitterness or just plain mad. God whom I speak with, if I should ever meet those people in soft clothing, the ones who took our clinic, let me be kind and polite, smile, then leave them alone. I will not hound them for rupees as some of the other HIV children do. It is You I can thank for being a lady-not even one curse word. Please let all these religious adults be like Kate in her goodness, forgiveness, in her way with the children, in her words which are always wise. I can plead this of You, my friend; I am weak and afraid, one who excites others to loathing, to Brahmans their future should they fail to achieve liberation. From one who, after all her vengeful acts, can still be heard by You in her ugly yet her own tiny shack.

Rupa Kumar was from India. If she had been born in America, her life would have been used as an example in the sermons of the pastors, who would have shed rivers of tears on her behalf- but when it came to bringing that mother and child into their large homes . . .

Bibliography

Cadeoux, C. John. The Early Christian Attitude to War. London: Headly Bros., 1919. Print

Gibbon, Edward. The Decline and Fall of the Roman Empire. London: Penguin Books, 2000. Print

Gibbon, Edward. The Decline and Fall of the Roman Empire. London: Random House, 2003. Print

Kierkegaard, Soren. A Kierkegaard Anthology. Princeton, New Jersey: Princeton University Press, 1946. Print

Printed in the United States
By Bookmasters